VICTOR
IN THE
RUBBLE

VICTOR
IN THE
RUBBLE

A SATIRE BY
ALEX FINLEY

Smiling Hippo Press

Victor in the Rubble
Copyright © 2016 by Alex Finley. All Rights Reserved.

For information about this title or to order other books and/or electronic media, contact the publisher:
Smiling Hippo Press
Washington, DC
SmilingHippoPress.com

ISBNs:
softcover: 978-0-9972510-0-5
eBook: 978-0-9972510-1-2

Printed in the United States of America
Cover and Interior design: 1106 Design

For Victor

Flabbergastipation:
When you are so in shock, you can't say shit.

CHAPTER ONE
AJAKAR, PIGALLO

"This is what terrorists call synergy," said Zed.

The burly chief of the CYA's Ajakar Station slapped his hand on a map of the world that was hanging on the wall. Victor jumped slightly at the sound but nodded at his new chief, a former Louisiana running back who took up most of the space in his office, and not just physically.

He and Zed were in Ajakar, the capital of the West African country of Pigallo, a former Italian colony that had joined its African brethren in a fit of independence in the 1960s.

"The Brotherhood is here." Zed pointed to the Republic of Zuzu, just north of Pigallo. Zuzu was a large country with a small population and was made up mostly of sand. It was proving an excellent hideout for a group that was quickly becoming a major threat to the United States.

"These rebels are joining forces with the Core, here." He pointed halfway across the world to Rubblestan, in the Middle East, where the United States had deployed 200,000 troops after the Core had attacked its homeland. "The Brotherhood is getting weapons, training, and money from the Core. And the Core gains an extended presence across Africa."

Zed turned away from the map and looked directly at his newest case officer. "Victor, why are you here?"

Victor stood in his worn out cargo pants and New York Fire Department T-shirt and summed up the attributes that would serve him well in the fight. "I'm a native Italian speaker. That'll give me some leverage dealing with our sources here. And I've got more than ten years of counterterrorism experience."

"No," Zed said. "It's because you're already fucked up." Zed returned to his desk and sat his solid frame down. "Ten years in Africa. You already know African logic. I don't have to explain to you why you can buy underwear, a toaster, and new wiper blades from the same guy at the intersection outside the embassy. Or why a sheep rides on top of a car. You already get that."

Victor leaned against the wall. "It's convenient shopping, and where else is the sheep going to ride?"

"Exactly!" Zed said, as he pounded his hand on the desk. "Now listen. Pigallo's president is a good partner for us. Director actually likes Wobuza and he's one of the least corrupt presidents on the continent."

"I suppose in Africa that's quite a compliment."

"He was democratically elected."

"Thirty-seven years ago, but go on."

"Director considers him a reliable partner and sees Pigallo as a strategic piece of our counterterrorism policy. We're right next door to Zuzu, and that's where the problems are brewing."

Victor turned back toward the map on the wall.

"Why the fuck are you still in here?" Zed growled at Victor. "Go find the bad guys."

Victor walked out of Zed's office, across the hall, and into the shark tank. The office where Victor and Ajakar Station's other case officers sat had no windows and its door was a foot-thick steel contraption. Victor felt he was walking into a giant safe. Several filing cabinets were in various states of disarray. Small magnetic signs that read "Open" or "Locked" were stuck to the filing drawers.

Victor pulled a map of West Africa off a bookshelf and sat at one of the free desks, where he unfolded the map and began studying the geography of the region.

This was one of his favorite parts of the job, when he had just arrived at a post and everything was new—new countries to discover, new cultures to decipher, and new targets to attain. *The potential.* That was what excited him. The possibility to crack targets Director thought impossible. All that still lay ahead. In two years, he knew, he would be cynical and jaded. Seeing a camel pulling a cart with a five-year-old on it selling counterfeit Chicago Bulls T-shirts would no longer be a novelty, but an annoyance.

He recalled when he had first landed in Somalia a few years back. Director was desperate to know what a particular chemical factory was manufacturing behind its barbed wire and thick, tall walls. At least three case officers had tried to get information from inside. All had failed. But Victor liked this kind of challenge. So when the chief told him the factory in Somalia should not be a target, since it was just a question of when, not if, Victor would fail, it was then Victor decided to prove his chief wrong.

Within a year Victor had secured a source inside the factory. A month after that, the inner workings of the factory, including what was being manufactured and who on the staff was banging whom, was being briefed on a regular basis to the National Security Council. Victor had been pleased.

But six months later, the intelligence gurus changed their priority matrix in preparation for the invasion of a different country, and Washington no longer viewed the fact that ricin was being produced in a lawless country like Somalia as an important detail. Director reprimanded Victor for spending so much time on a useless target.

Six months after that, Director reprimanded Victor yet again, when ricin from Somalia was discovered in a New York City apartment and Congress wanted answers about why the intelligence community didn't foresee the possibility of a ricin attack.

But for now, thought Victor as he pored over the map of West Africa, Pigallo remained full of promise and Victor, despite himself, remained dedicated to the mission. The son of an Italian mother and French-American father and raised in Paris, Victor had long ago chosen his side.

"You must be Victor."

Victor looked up and saw a short man approaching him with an outstretched hand. He was thick at the waist and had pulled his pants up and over his belly with a belt cinched just under his man boobs. His short pants revealed white tube socks and black rubber-soled shoes.

"Hi, yes, Victor Caro." Victor stood up to shake his hand.

"Welcome. I'm Joseph, the support officer. I'm here to make sure you have everything you need to do your job. I'm just as devastated as the next guy about those attacks. If you need anything, you let me know. Anything."

"Thanks," Victor said, sitting back down. Joseph's cheerful face turned suddenly dour.

"Is this where you're planning to sit?"

"Yep." Victor pulled a lever under the seat of his chair and dropped down a few inches, then pumped himself back up.

Joseph took a deep breath, pressed his lips together, and glanced briefly around the tank. "That's a GS-15 chair. And that's a GS-15 desk."

Victor raised his eyebrows, but did not blink.

Joseph shook his head in annoyance. "You are a GS-13." He said it as if it were a disease. "This furniture is above your pay grade, according to regulation 68-F1 as amended. Technically, I could get fired for letting you sit there."

"There are furniture regulations?" Victor asked. He glanced around the shark tank at the various desks and chairs and then looked back at Joseph. "And you know them?"

"I'm gonna let it go, for now," Joseph said, as if he were doing Victor an enormous favor. "But keep it quiet."

Victor stifled a laugh. Hardly anything the United States government did anymore was kept quiet.

"I'll figure out a place to switch you later," Joseph said before walking out.

Victor sat in his GS-15 chair, suddenly much more aware of its ergonomic comfort. He switched on his computer, which gave him its default greeting, "Welcome to the CYA."

CHAPTER TWO
NUAKABATU, REPUBLIC OF ZUZU

Omar al-Suqqit stared at the blinking cursor on the screen and read the top of the form, "Application to Swear *Bay'at* to the Core." A small icon in the corner revealed that this was the first of forty-seven pages. He sighed.

For years, Omar had been trying to push his small free-dom-fighting group, the Brotherhood, onto the international stage. The group had begun as a ragtag gathering of Zuzuan outcasts who felt disenfranchised and aimed to bring down the country's autocratic elite, represented at the top by the dictator Yaya Tata. Tata's grasp on Zuzu's peanut industry had made him and his friends extraordinarily wealthy. While Tata built himself a scale-size replica of the Palazzo Medici in the middle of the desert, complete with a private runway and koi pond filled with goldfish, the rest of the country's citizens struggled to eke out a subsistence living. They had no schools, no hospitals, and no opportunity.

Among Tata's entourage was Omar's father, a highly successful peanut farmer who had grown his business into one of Africa's major peanut exporters. Omar was the only child of his father's third, and favorite, wife. But when it was discovered that Omar suffered from peanut allergies, his father's plans to pass the peanut empire to him had been dashed and Omar had become lost in his father's peanut gallery of forty-six children. Feeling ostracized, Omar turned to the Brotherhood.

Over several years, he built a reputation as one of the group's best soldiers. He organized peanut smashing rallies in Zuzu's capital, Nuakabatu, and he and his comrades would throw peanuts at Zuzu's political leaders whenever they gave a public speech. (Omar just organized these peanut-throwing festivities. Given his allergies, he couldn't actually participate.) He created a smuggling network through West Africa, trading in weapons, cars, and diamonds, and excelled at abductions, netting the Brotherhood millions of dollars and making it one of the wealthiest fighting groups in Africa.

Omar even did a stint in Rubblestan's war, where brothers like him were fighting a different dictator. Rubblestan had become the unifying rallying call against all oppression and brothers from around the world flocked there to join the struggle under the tutelage of the Core, one of the main fighting groups that hoped to spread its religious revolution across the globe. Omar trained and fought alongside some of the Core's best commanders. He returned to Zuzu a hardened fighter who had earned the respect of the Brotherhood's other members.

He also returned with a new perspective on the struggle in general, a perspective developed over weeks of bonding with other fighters in Rubblestan. Omar had come to blame outside forces, rather than his own country's elite, for the oppression suffered in

Zuzu. Specifically, he shook his finger at the United States' enormous appetite for peanuts. It was the Americans' consumption of his country's peanuts that propped up the autocratic elite and gave them the resources to tyrannize the people of Zuzu. And it wasn't just Zuzu, Omar understood. Dictators across the world held on to power using American money.

This was bigger than overthrowing Tata now. Omar wanted a role in the global struggle. Once the Core carried out its grandiose attacks on the United States, Omar knew it was time to make his move. The Brotherhood would swear loyalty to the Core and, under Omar's command, would step onto the international freedom-fighting scene.

His main ideological opponent was Dr. Zawiki, one of the founders of the Brotherhood and the architect of the group's focus on terrorizing Zuzu's government. But Zawiki was a mediocre orator who had never distinguished himself on the battlefield. Worse, he lacked a crucial characteristic of a leader: he had no charisma. He was fat and had hair in all the wrong places, and he wore funny glasses. Most noteworthy, he had never been able to shake his nickname, Zawiki al-Liki, which he had acquired in an unsavory childhood incident involving a goat and his testicles.

Omar, on the other hand, was tall and handsome. When he wasn't near peanuts, he had nearly flawless skin. He also had a certain commanding presence. And having grown up with the elites and then shunning that easy lifestyle gave him additional status among the rank and file.

With resolve, Omar sipped his cup of chai and started at the top of the application.

Applicant's Father's Name: Ali al-Suqqit
Applicant's Date of Birth: 1972, rainy season
Applicant's Beard Length: 28 centimeters
When wearing a vest, do you tend to run toward a
building or away from it?
Swear in writing three times to hate the West.

Omar looked at the icon in the corner of the application. He still had forty-six pages to go. He leaned back on his chair and stretched and then poised his fingers over the keyboard. After a deep breath, he began tapping away and thus took the first step in the long process of taking down Western Civilization.

***

A month later, Omar found himself waiting at a desert landing strip in Zuzu, holding up a hand-written sign that said, "The Core." The leadership in Rubblestan had deemed the Brotherhood worthy of unity with the global struggle and, after the Brotherhood had paid its membership dues through a hawala office, agreed to send a representative to Zuzu to welcome the Brotherhood into the Core's fold. Omar watched the plane approach and covered his eyes as it kicked up sand upon landing. He caught his breath and tried to temper his excitement. Sand was still swirling when the plane came to a stop. The door opened and the stairs were released. A sharply dressed representative from the Core's headquarters in Rubblestan appeared at the plane's door. He had a phone to his ear and was talking loudly. He spotted Omar's sign and confidently stepped down the stairs.

Omar stepped forward to welcome the representative, who shook his hand dismissively and kept talking on the phone as he and Omar climbed onto a camel and Omar instructed the camel driver where to go.

"Tell the imam London is already taken," the representative said into the phone. "Hamburg, too. We need someone in Milan." He paused. "I know he speaks English and German, but those spots are filled. It's Milan or he waits till someone else gets renditioned." He continued for quite some time as the camel made its way to where Omar's Brotherhood brethren were waiting to hear about the union of their group with the Core.

They arrived finally at an isolated tent and slid off the camel just as the Core representative finished telling his secretary that the airline had failed to offer a halal meal and would she please fix that for the return flight. He strode into the tent, leaving Omar to carry his bag, and began fumbling with computer cables while Omar deposited the bag in a corner and poured a small glass of mint tea for his visitor. He stepped up on the stage, where a screen was showing the Core's logo, and looked down at the carpet where Omar's lieutenants were perched. He sipped the tea and cleared his throat.

"Welcome, everyone. Welcome. I am Mohamed. Not to be confused with Muhammed, or Muhamad. We in Rubblestan are very pleased to welcome you into the Core family. As you all know, jihad is a communal effort and you, as the Core in the Desert, will play a key role in the administration of jihad in western and northern Africa. Through you, we hope to attain a qualitative leap in jihadist action globally. Core Central in Rubblestan will help guide you and will endure to smooth any creases between all Core groups as you each pursue international jihad."

Omar looked at his men, who seemed engaged. In the back row, Omar saw Zawiki, his pudgy fingers wrapped around a pistachio donut.

"Our organization has grown so quickly," Mohamed said, as the slide on the screen changed. "This is very positive, of course, but it also means we have had to alter our pathway to absorb our flourishing success. For example," he continued, "Next slide, please. Next slide. For example, our martyrdom program has exceeded expectations and experienced fifty percent growth over the same period last year." He looked back at the men while they took in this statistic. "The down side, of course, is that it is very difficult to write lessons learned from our suicide bomber program. We also may soon run out of virgins in Paradise."

Omar's men let out a collective groan. Omar glanced around nervously. The promise of luscious purity was one of the main reasons he had attracted so many young followers.

Mohamed pleaded for calm, making soothing motions with his hands and assuring the men with soft eyes and nods of his head that this was not as bad as it seemed. He continued with an authoritative voice, "For now, at least, we can still offer seventy-two technical virgins. These ladies may be a little more worldly, but I assure you they are more than capable of satisfying your needs."

Omar's men murmured their agreement and seemed to accept this, albeit reluctantly.

"But given the current rates of attrition, this, too, may not be sustainable, so we encourage you to sign up for this program now, while we can still guarantee benefits."

After Mohamed had finished his presentation, members of the newly named Core in the Desert milled around the tent chatting and catching up on their latest projects. As Omar was approaching Mohamed, Zawiki stepped in front of him and thrust his hand at the Core representative.

"Thanks for coming, Mr. Mohamed. I really like your ideas," Zawiki said, taking Mohamed's hand. He didn't let go. "I think this merger is going to be great for all of us."

Omar inserted himself into the conversation. "Yes, Mr. Mohamed. A great presentation."

Zawiki cut Omar off. "I wanted to run an idea by you. Something I think could be a real positive contribution to this partnership."

Mohamed responded with a smile, "Please, tell me."

"I'm working on a new software program that I think could provide real value-added to the jihadi struggle."

"What does the program do?"

"It creates boxes."

"What for?"

"To check," Zawiki said. "To keep us organized." A crumb clinging to Zawiki's beard fell to the floor.

"Does it do anything else?"

"No. It just creates boxes to check. It's quite forward leaning."

"Indeed," the envoy said. "That's exactly the kind of new thinking we're looking for." Mohamed turned to Omar and, pointing at Zawiki, said, "We'll be keeping an eye on this one."

"We certainly will," Omar agreed. He took Mohamed by the elbow and guided him away from Zawiki. Omar saw Zawiki pick up the crumb from the floor and eat it. "Mr. Mohamed, as I explained to you in our application, General bin Fuqin, the head of the Zuzuan Army, has assured me he would be quite sympathetic to our cause, if perhaps we could help him secure Zuzu from that dictator Tata." Both men sat down in a corner of the tent and one of Omar's lieutenants brought them a bowl of hummus with pita slices on the side.

"Indeed," the envoy said, dipping the bread in the smashed chickpeas. "Core Central Leadership was intrigued by the idea. We would have more room to maneuver here in the desert, helping us to advance the jihad globally." He sipped his tea. "What would you need to support General bin Fuqin's coup d'état?"

"Some weapons and some men. Maybe some money. Our treasury has decreased slightly, as the men are starting to find routine abductions rather dull. But I am thinking further ahead, to the next move. With bin Fuqin in place and freedom to train and move, I plan to target the United States."

"We're always pleased to hear that," Mohamed said. "Core Central will be there to lead you through."

He and Omar shook hands. Omar was so encouraged by the meeting he could feel the excitement welling up from his breast. Finally, his group would be an international player. "Just one thing," the Core envoy said. "Be sure to save your receipts."

CHAPTER THREE
AJAKAR, PIGALLO

Victor was sipping his morning coffee when he heard, "Caro! Get your ass in here!"

"Yeah, boss?" Victor poked his head around Zed's office door.

"Sit."

Victor did.

"It finally happened," Zed said. "They've been talking about it for years. The big attacks were the catalyst to make it a reality."

Victor had no idea what Zed was talking about, so not saying anything seemed like his best option.

"The Intelligence Über Director," Zed declared in a booming voice. He looked at Victor with anticipation, as though expecting him to display a visceral reaction to the news. Victor looked at Zed with a blank expression. "Do you ever read cables?" Zed asked.

"Did you bring me to Ajakar to read cables?"

"Fair point. But you're kind of missing out by not reading this one. The Intelligence Über Director. The IÜD. The big attacks were blamed on a 'systemic failure.' That allowed us to place blame everywhere and nowhere at once. The IÜD is here to fix all that. It will coordinate cross-agency cooperation and cooperate with cross-agency coordination, to make sure we are all coordinating and cooperating in what shall henceforth be called the Total War on Terror. The TWOT."

"They probably should have market tested the acronyms."

"They also renamed the Division of Operations. We are now the National Operations Branch."

"Are they changing how we operate?"

"No. Just changing the name. And a lot of software codes. Probably a few million dollars to change the software codes to reflect the new name. And the logo. We get a new logo. But the IÜD, yes, might make our work a little harder. I'm sorry, easier. As your boss I am supposed to tell you it will make everything easier, because now we get to coordinate and cooperate with everyone else in the government."

"It's insane," said Victor. "We're in the middle of a crisis and they're recreating the wheel."

"Even better, young Victor. They're recreating the square wheel, lest we find the current system of catching terrorists not enough of a challenge. Speaking of which, you're going to Zuzu."

"I am?"

"You are. One of the Core's communications men popped up on the radar up there. You gotta meet with Source Abdul and find out why. Take the Land Rover. Keys are in the safe."

"The Land Rover doesn't have any license plates."

Zed disappeared behind his desk and dug through the bottom drawer. Victor heard some clanging and Zed reappeared with two license plates. "Here, take these."

Victor grabbed them from his chief and went to pack his bags.

CHAPTER FOUR
NUAKABATU, REPUBLIC OF ZUZU

Omar hurried around his tent, fluffing the pillows and cushions and adjusting the rugs. He had never welcomed an army general before, and he knew how important first impressions were. At exactly ten o'clock, a young man in an army uniform appeared at Omar's tent door to announce the general's arrival.

"Please come in," Omar said.

General bin Fuqin was tall and broad. He looked as solid as a steel wall. His hair was dark and curly, trimmed close to his head. He had on an immaculate army uniform, and he wore dark Ray-Ban Aviator sunglasses, which he left on, even inside. He was flanked on all sides by an armed entourage of young boys whose ripped pants and dirty T-shirts were incongruous next to the general's sharpness. Omar and bin Fuqin both sat down on a carpet. A silver tea set on a giant tray rested between them. The young boys formed a semi-circle behind the general.

"I've heard you had a visitor from Rubblestan," bin Fuqin started. "And I received your proposal suggesting you and I work together."

"We are prepared to help you take over Zuzu. We can provide you with weapons, men, and money." Omar hoped he was telling the general the truth. Getting receipts on the black market was proving to be an obstacle, and Omar wasn't sure how much money he could advance to General bin Fuqin out of his own coffers. But he knew how hard it was to secure a meeting with the general, so when the opportunity had arisen, he had chosen to seize it, rather than wait for a clarification from Rubblestan.

"And in return?" the general asked.

"You let us be. You don't bother us, and we won't bother you."

Bin Fuqin sipped his tea with a slurp. "I like your tea," he said, wiping his mouth. "And I like you." He snapped his fingers fiercely and one of the boys stepped forward with a map, which he rolled out on the floor in front of Omar and the general. Without further ceremony, the two men laid out their plans.

CHAPTER FIVE
SOMEWHERE BETWEEN PIGALLO AND
THE REPUBLIC OF ZUZU

It was when he saw the soldier running after his car that Victor figured something might be wrong. He stopped the car and out of a dust cloud emerged a young Pigallese border control officer. He came to Victor's window and coughed. A small burst of dust came out of his mouth. "Signore!" he panted. "The border." He pointed back in the direction Victor had just come from.

Victor looked around at the sand, plants, and rocks. "There's a border here?"

The soldier kept pointing, so Victor put the car in reverse and hit the pedal, leaving the soldier in another cloud of dirt. About a hundred yards back, nestled between two boulders, was a tiny shack. Pigallese Customs and Border Control.

Victor entered the shack and approached a man in an impeccable dark green uniform. He sat rigid behind a desk, his back straight and both arms resting on the immaculate workspace. He wore thick, black-rimmed glasses. "Welcome. Passport please."

Victor placed his documents on the desk. The man slowly and meticulously looked through each page, scrutinizing each visa before deliberately turning to the next page. Then suddenly, with a flourish, he whipped out his rubber stamp and stamped Victor's passport five times with the same stamp, *bam bam bam bam bam!* He finished his masterpiece with a whimsical signature that connected all five stamps and filled the entire passport page. "Safe travels, signore. Please come back to Pigallo soon." He handed Victor his documents and Victor turned to walk out. The soldier who had chased his car was sitting in a corner still coughing up dust.

Victor returned to his car and drove on, slowly this time and fully on the lookout for whatever might serve as the border shack marking the entry to the Republic of Zuzu. He crossed a river and then saw it, two piles of cinderblocks with corrugated roofs, and a tree trunk lying across the road. He got out of the car and looked around. Not a hint of life stirred.

Victor tentatively entered the first worn-down border house where an older, worn-down soldier dressed in fatigues was asleep on a thin, worn-down mattress on a sandy, worn-down floor. The mattress was only long enough for his upper body; his legs sprawled on the dirt floor. Victor stood there waiting, wondering if he should wake him up, and if so, how. He thought to knock on the door, except there was no door. He coughed, and coughed again, until finally the soldier opened his eyes and looked at Victor, completely annoyed.

He grunted and led Victor over to a broken desk, shuffling in his flip-flops. He sat down on a broken chair. A calendar from 1998 hung above him. Victor sat down across from the wary man, unsure if the wobbly chair with no back would hold him. As the soldier opened Victor's passport, another border guard came in the hut, seemingly out of nowhere. He dug in, towering over Victor, just as the first guard said with a grin, "Your visa is fake."

For a moment, Victor imagined himself becoming the subject of one of those blurbs at the bottom of an inside page of a newspaper, about some random American who has gone missing under vague conditions in a far off country no American has ever heard of. Some latte-drinking banker in New York would read it and say, "What a shame, but how exotic!" then quickly turn the page.

The idea annoyed Victor. He determined not to allow these Zuzuan officials to turn him and his imperative work of chasing terrorists into fodder. "I'm here on official business for the government of the United States," Victor pronounced. "My government would never falsify a visa." *And when we do,* he thought, *we do it well.*

The two guards looked at each other wondering what to do next. Clearly, the false visa strategy had worked for them in the past.

"We don't allow people wearing brown pants to enter the country," one said. The second guard nodded in agreement.

Victor looked at his khakis and then back up at the guard as if to say, "Are you fucking serious?" *There is no way I'm going to pay this guy a bribe,* Victor thought. But he needed to get to Zuzu's capital, Nuakabatu, without raising suspicion or causing a diplomatic incident.

"Of course, you can buy a special brown-pants waiver visa," the first guard said.

"My pants are khaki."

"Then I most certainly cannot allow you to enter. Khakis are strictly forbidden on Tuesdays. Unless, of course, you are interested in a Khaki Tuesday visa. For you, my friend, I can process this very fast, for an extra fee, of course."

"My friend," Victor said, getting up and sitting on the edge of the desk, which teetered beneath him. Victor placed his hand on the guard's shoulder. "I'm here to bring business to your country. Money. You get that? *Money*. So your government can pay you. A real salary. Not a little money here and there. But a *real salary*. When is the last time you were paid? Honestly, wouldn't you like a new mattress?" Victor motioned to the thin, dirty mat on the floor where the guard had been sleeping. "A full-length mattress? Your government should provide it. That's why I'm here."

The soldier was so overwhelmed at the thought of a full-length mattress, Victor thought the soldier was going to cry. Instead, the soldier took out a red inkpad and a date stamp. He fiddled with the numbers on the stamp to get it to the correct year. It took so long Victor figured no one had passed through this particular border post since 1982. Once he finally got the stamp to the twenty-first century, the guard pushed it on the inkpad with a thud. He looked at the stamp. He slammed it into the inkpad again and looked. He spit on the inkpad and put the stamp in the moist spot and at last stamped Victor's passport. He then picked up a broken pen and licked the tip. He wrote a full paragraph in the passport under the stamp, declaring officially and with honor and under government permission and with diplomacy that Victor Caro had the right, nay, the *need* to enter Zuzu, and Zuzu was privileged to have him.

The guard stood up and handed Victor his passport with a hopeful smile. He then threw his arms around Victor and squeezed warmly. He released Victor, nodded once, and patted Victor's shoulder as Victor walked out.

Victor crossed to the second hut where a third official had to officialize the official stamp he had just received from the first two officials. This soldier was also lying on a mattress on the floor when Victor entered, prepared to give the same speech again if needed. The official had wrapped a wet towel around his head as protection against the heat. Without a word, he shuffled to the desk and signed off on Victor's stamps. Then he looked up and mumbled, "If you have a chance to bring some tea, that would be nice." He shuffled outside to roll the tree trunk out of the road.

Victor returned to his car and waved to the soldiers as he officially crossed the border and entered Zuzu. The soldier who had hugged him waved back enthusiastically, a look of hope illuminating his face. From his rearview mirror, he could see the soldier still waving until he faded out of sight.

Victor passed over another river and assumed he was on what Zed had called the dam road, since the river flowed into a dam that provided occasional electricity to both Zuzu and Pigallo.

"Once you're on the dam road, head east until you hit the paved road," Zed had told him.

"Which paved road?" Victor had asked.

"*The* paved road. There's only one in the country."

Victor glanced to his right at the grassy bushes, the last vestiges of the marshy area off the river. To his left, a very hot, large, and sandy expanse of land melted toward the horizon. He went east.

Victor maneuvered the car along the dirt road, trying to match his tires with the car tracks that had been left by previous passers-by, and waded through packs of wild camels, who sat lazily in the middle of the road and appeared to smile as they silently conveyed the message, "There's no fucking way I'm going to move in this heat."

Soon, the grass faded out and Victor was surrounded only by beige sand that was spotted by a few boulders. Brown-green bushes speckled the landscape here and there. At points, the sand turned pink, creating a Martian scene, broken with sudden strikes of gray and black, as if the sun had gotten too hot at that spot and scorched it completely.

Victor checked the outside temperature gauge, which was rising steadily toward forty-four degrees Celsius. Outside he saw nothing but sand and immovable camels. He leaned over to grab a piece of gum and looked back at the road just in time to see a man walking in the opposite direction. *Where on Earth did he come from? Where on Earth is he going? And why the fuck is he wearing a wool cap?* Victor passed him and stared.

After about two hours and several near collisions with camels, Victor took an inventory of the water bottles in the back of the car. He wondered how long he could survive in the desert if the car were to break down, and whether he possessed the fortitude to kill a camel or that man in a wool cap in order to have food to survive. He patted a small cooler on the passenger seat for reassurance. Inside was a kilogram of feta cheese that Victor had put on ice like a human organ. The ambassador in Nuakabatu had asked the embassy in Ajakar to please send feta with the next official who was coming to Zuzu—because what better way to transport cheese than on ice in a cooler nine hours in the desert? Victor knew that if he were to disappear in this ocean of sand, no one would miss him. But he figured the ambassador would miss his cheese and would eventually send out the Marines to find it if it didn't make it to the ambassador's residence in due time.

Victor passed a hand-written POLICE sign that stuck out of the sand at a crooked angle. He slowed down when he saw a soldier who looked like he was melting on the ground under a blue plastic bag, whose corners he had attached to four sticks to provide him a few inches of shade. With the tiniest movement of his hand and a clear effort not to move too much in the heat, the soldier simply waved Victor on.

The hours and camels ticked by. Victor ate without stopping, bread and cookie crumbs flying around as he bounced along the track. The gas gauge went down. The temperature gauge went up. And then he saw another man in a wool cap, sitting under a tree. Victor stopped the car, rolled down the window, and was hit by a massive wave of heat that physically knocked his head back.

When he had regained his composure, Victor said to the man, "Excuse me, I'm looking for the paved road to Nuakabatu."

"Signore," he said, incredibly brightly, considering the spirit-crushing heat. "You have two choices. Continue this direction about nine more kilometers, or go left here. When you see the big rock, turn right. Go past the three tents, so they are on your left, and continue past the tree. And there you will find the road."

Victor thanked him and quickly rolled up his window. He turned left, then right at the rock, passed the tents and the tree and bounced onto a road. He let out a small laugh of joy. *It's like Zuzu's autobahn!* He swerved around a giant pothole. He headed north for about five minutes, and then stopped to double check the map, which confirmed that the country was endowed with only one paved highway. He looked up. The road was kind of paved. It was more like globs of tar had occasionally been dropped in between potholes. *This must be it!* He pressed the accelerator.

He turned to dodge another pothole, bumped off the road, and swerved again to avoid hitting a dead camel, its limbs rigid and its body bloated from the heat. Along the road he passed a few huts and houses with partially completed walls of cinderblocks, sometimes with a roof, sometimes not. With time, the clumps of people and huts began getting closer and closer together, and Victor realized he must be approaching the great capital of Nuakabatu.

Finally! He was eager to stretch his legs and rinse out some of the sand now coating his teeth. He looked over at the feta cheese, slapped his face to help wake himself up and then concentrated once again on the road, where he soon realized the clumps of huts were thinning out. *Fucking hell. Did I miss it? How could I miss a capital city?*

He pulled into the first gas station he had seen in the country, figuring it meant he couldn't be too far from civilization. Before he could come to a full stop, he found himself surrounded, as a group of people descended on his car, tapping on the windows and doors, holding up chewing gum and counterfeit Marlboro cigarettes for sale. "I know, I know," Victor said, as he opened his window and tried to calm the gaggle. "I'm your excitement for the week, aren't I? A lost white guy. Nuakabatu? Where's Nuakabatu?" He switched into Italian. "I'm trying to go to Nuakabatu."

Fingers shot up in all directions amongst shouts of "Yes! Nuakabatu! That way!"

Victor did a quick survey and decided the majority of the fingers seemed to be pointing back in the direction he had just come from. "Seriously? That group of huts? That's the capital?" he asked.

The people nodded eagerly, still pointing in different directions. He bought a pack of gum and carefully extricated the car from the agitated mob. He then circled back and turned off the road to enter Nuakabatu.

The city had three stoplights and eight partially paved roads. He looked at a hand-drawn map of the city that Zed had given him while saying helpfully, "No map company could be bothered to make a map of that shithole." He found his way to his hotel, which looked like a worn-down Howard Johnson's with furniture from the sixties. Victor moaned as he stretched his legs out of the car, and then he headed straight to the bar to ask the barman to replace the ice in the cooler to ensure the feta he was trafficking wouldn't go bad.

In his room, Victor stepped into the shower, eager to scrub off the layers of dirt that had come in through the car vents and accumulated on his skin during the nine-hour drive. He turned the knob, waiting for the powerful spray to bring him long-awaited cleanliness. Instead, drops of cold water trickled from a hose that was attached to the faucet and duct-taped to the wall of the tub. Victor rubbed each drop into his skin and the mud slowly melted off.

Feeling only slightly refreshed, Victor headed out to Casablanca, which Zed had informed him was the only restaurant in the Islamic country's capital that served alcohol. Victor was dreaming of a cold beer as he drove through town, glancing occasionally at Zed's map, making his way to the restaurant. He turned a corner, looked up, and saw with dismay that he was back at his hotel. "What the fuck?" he said. "It's not like this is a huge fucking metropolis!" He slammed his hand on the steering wheel, irritated to be back in the car after his daylong road trip and eager to quench his thirst.

"Excuse me," he said to a man in a white robe and blue headdress who was standing idly on the road. "Casablanca?"

The man gave Victor a calm and wise smile. "Go down this paved road, and then turn left on the dirt road after the spot where the black goat is attached to a pole in the ground."

Two minutes later, Victor was sipping a warm, watered-down beer.

CHAPTER SIX
NUAKABATU, REPUBLIC OF ZUZU

Despite the hard bed in Nuakabatu's only hotel, Victor had slept deeply after the long drive and warm beer. He woke up early the next morning to signal a meeting with Abdul, a member of Zuzu's national police force and a well-established CYA asset who maintained a network of contacts that allowed him to provide good information on the growing number of extremists in Zuzu. The signal for the meeting was a letter that began "Dear George" and contained the phrase "The desert wind has been cold." The letter was to be placed in a particular post office box in Nuakabatu's post office. The post office was a one-room shack with a corrugated tin roof in the middle of a sandy plot of land across from the hotel. Victor noticed he still had sand stuck under his fingernails as he wrote out the letter, stuffed it in the envelope, and asked the man in the service window for a stamp.

"Two hundred fifty chifas," the man said.

Victor handed him a thousand-chifa note.

"Exact change only, sir."

Victor checked his pockets. Nothing. "I don't have exact change."

"Exact change only."

Having exact change was not taught at spy school and Victor imagined that if word of this little mishap ever made it back to Director, the minions in Washington would quickly develop an entire course on making change in foreign currencies. It would require all case officers to carry with them, at all times, at least ten of each coin from the country they were in, as well as from all surrounding countries in a 500-mile radius.

"Just keep the change," Victor told him, at which point the man miraculously made change and pocketed 750 chifas for himself.

***

That evening, Victor made his way to what had once been the parking lot of a now-defunct cinema to meet Abdul. A group of nomads had stopped there for the night. Two camels were tied to a fence. The group, in flourishing blue robes, sat around a fire cooking kebabs and drinking tea. A dog lay a few feet away; alive or dead, Victor couldn't tell. Other than the light of the fire, the lot was pitch-black. Victor adjusted the Boston Red Sox cap he was wearing and took a sip from his water bottle. He had never met Abdul. The combination of the hat and bottle was the sign that would allow the source to recognize his new handler.

Across the lot, Victor saw a car with its motor running, but its lights off. It moved toward him a little. Victor adjusted his cap and took another sip of water. The car moved closer. Victor walked to it. *This must be Abdul.*

Victor leaned toward the passenger side window and said in Italian, "Excuse me, do you know where I can get some more water?"

The dark face inside was hidden in the shadows, but its voice replied, "That water is a miracle of nature."

Victor slid into the car and Abdul started driving.

"You are Harold's replacement?" Abdul asked.

"Yes, he had to go back to the United States. Do you know what to say if we're stopped?"

"I have simply taken pity on a lost white boy who shouldn't have been out walking alone here at night. It's dangerous, you know. I am driving you back to your hotel."

"Good, now what information do you have for me? I think Harold outlined what we're interested in during your last meeting with him."

"It's true what I said. With your baseball hat in that parking lot, you didn't exactly blend in. Maybe next time you should go to the local market beforehand. Buy a local hat."

"Thank you for your advice. Now—"

"Because you speak Italian very well for an American. But that hat—"

"Could we move on to the substance, please? We don't have much time."

"Here." Abdul grabbed a stack of papers from the backseat and threw them in Victor's lap. "The Brotherhood is planning to overthrow Tata's government. They have the support of the military, including General bin Fuqin. We think Omar al-Suqqit is behind the coup plot, or at least financing it. He has kept a low profile, but we know he is a powerful force in the Brotherhood. He met recently with Mohamed bin Mohamed, who came from Rubblestan and is a known communications officer for the Core. In a raid on a Brotherhood camp last week, we found these."

Abdul pulled out a stack of papers that included maps and notes outlining the coup plan.

Victor considered the implications of this information. Zuzu's President Tata was an ally of President Wobuza back in Pigallo. While Tata spoke publicly of sovereignty and bashed the idea of foreign influence, privately he welcomed the money flow from the West and passed information to Wobuza to help both countries maintain security in their common border areas.

But Tata also understood the strong religious currents that flowed through his country. He had nationalized much of the peanut industry years ago, and he used most of the huge influx of foreign currency that came from the West's peanut consumption to pay off the religious leadership to keep groups like the Brotherhood at bay and allow him some peace to rule. Without Tata, Zuzu would certainly become an enormous desert playground for the Core and their subsidiaries. This was precisely the synergy Zed had been talking about.

Only a few minutes later, Abdul pulled up next to the black goat chained to the post at the corner. Victor got out. "Thanks, Abdul." They shook hands through the open window. "I'll be back in a few weeks." Abdul drove off. Victor walked around the corner to Casablanca, stuffing the documents into his backpack.

***

The next morning, Victor went to the embassy to meet with the Ambassador Extraordinary and Plenipotentiary of the United States of America to the Republic of Zuzu. Paul Nash, a career foreign service officer, lived in a compound within the main embassy compound, surrounded by a lovely tennis court and a cool swimming pool. Victor wondered whom he had pissed off to be named ambassador to such a shithole. The rumor was that Nash hardly went out, and when he did, it was with Zuzu's President Tata and his cronies. How much he understood about what was happening on the other side of the bougainvillea was a matter of speculation within the offices of the CYA.

"Come on in and have a seat." Nash remained seated behind his enormous desk and motioned to a chair. Victor reached across to shake his hand, but Nash was looking down at his papers. Victor sat down and held out the feta cheese.

"I brought this for you from Ajakar."

Nash took it, still without looking at Victor but with a nod of acknowledgement, and set it aside. He inhaled deeply through his nose, and then exhaled with a puff. He finally looked directly at Victor.

"What are you doing up here in my country?" He had a thick Texas accent. He leaned back and glared at Victor.

"I believe Zed explained to you, we have some concerns about the Brotherhood. We have evidence that their leader, Omar al-Suqqit, recently met with Mohamed bin Mohamed from Rubblestan. Zed sent me to find out why."

"You guys are always making something out of nothing, aren't you?" Nash's twang was palpable, as he leaned his elbows on his desk and shook his head at Victor. "The Brotherhood has been around for ages. It has a few religious overtones, but mostly they play sports, kind of like the YMCA. They go camping, for Christ's sake. Sure, they participate in a bit of civil disobedience every now and then. Peanut butter graffiti, that kind of thing. But mostly they're harmless students going through a rebellious phase."

"We have reason to believe the Brotherhood is partnering with the Core. They've also been in contact with the military here in Zuzu. We have reports that al-Suqqit has been meeting with bin Fuqin."

"Now, you listen to me." Nash wagged a long, bony finger at Victor. "This here is my territory, and nothing happens here without me knowing about it. Tata doesn't take a shit unless I tell him to. And I pay the military's salary. General bin Fuqin is a close friend of mine and a regular at my annual holiday party."

"You can't invite him, sir."

"Who the hell are you to tell me who I can and cannot invite to my party?"

"We have information from a very reliable source that bin Fuqin is assisting al-Suqqit and vice versa. They're planning a coup d'état. They're planning to overthrow Tata."

"Son, you need to stop hanging out in the streets and start talking to people who actually know what's going on. Tata has assured me his government is secure."

"How does he know that? He never leaves his palace."

"You're in over your head here, and I'll tell Zed that. Now, I think you should head back to Pigallo and stick your nose in their business. Stay out of my country. And don't you go reporting any of that crudités crap back to your Director. Any reporting you put out better go through me first." In an instant, he put on a big grin and said, "Thanks for visiting. Bye now." He went back to looking at the papers on his desk.

Victor stood up and walked out without another word. On the desk of the ambassador's secretary, he noticed a framed newspaper profile of Nash. He picked it up and read the article, which revealed that Nash had been an embassy officer in Gabimbia when that country had had its coup d'état. He had been held hostage by rebels for a week before they let him go. "I was surprised when they came into the embassy compound," he had told the newspaper. Victor feared lightning was going to strike twice for this guy, and Nash was too busy waving around a metal rod to realize the approaching danger. He needed to discuss the issue with Zed, who had more authority to tell Nash off. Victor returned to his hotel for a last hose shower before the camel-filled drive back to Ajakar.

***

With the coup d'état only a few days away, Omar was stressed. His men were tired from the joint training sessions with bin Fuqin's soldiers but also eager to get on with the action. Their pent up energy was making them restless and Omar had noticed some of them spending a little too much time alone behind the tent. On top of that, he was racing the clock to get delivery of a case of rocket-propelled grenades. Core Central in Rubblestan had transferred Omar's usual arms dealer to the Core in the Peninsula, another group that had recently sworn *Bay'at* to the Core, and the new guy seemed to have gotten lost in the desert. Omar didn't have the money to pay him anyway. He called in Zawiki, who was in the next tent over helping with the final preparations.

"Zawiki!" Omar called out a second time, and finally Zawiki shuffled into the main tent, licking frosting off his fingers. "Where do we stand with the funding from Rubblestan?"

"We're working on it, but so far we haven't been able to set up a hawala system between Zuzu and Rubblestan. There's some disagreement on what exchange rate we should use."

"What are you doing to fix the problem?"

Zawiki shrugged. "Waiting for Core Central to get back to me."

"That's it?"

"And eating some pastries Karim brought in. Would you like one?"

Omar dismissed Zawiki and rushed out of the tent to the post office, where his cousin Assim worked. On Omar's instructions, Assim called his wife's uncle who ran a hawala stand in Rubblestan. The uncle, after asking about each and every one of Assim's family members, sent a runner to Core Central's headquarters, and within fifteen minutes, Omar had his money.

CHAPTER SEVEN
AJAKAR, PIGALLO

After nine sweaty hours in his car, Victor was elated to see the village that marked the outskirts of Ajakar. His joy was short-lived, however, as the traffic came to a standstill. Until now, the return trip had been generally uneventful. His border crossing between Zuzu and Pigallo had gone more smoothly. To begin, he knew to stop this time. When he entered the hut where the man on the small mattress was snoozing, Victor plunked down a bag of sugar, a bag of tea, and his passport. Without a word, the sleepy soldier spit on his inkpad and stamped Victor's documents.

Victor massaged his neck and tried to see over the cars in front of him to discover the hold up. Maybe a passing car had killed a goat and a melee had broken out between the driver and the goat's owner. Or maybe the locals were walking through the cars to sell their fruit, blissfully unaware that people in cars tended to want to go somewhere, rather than sit still in an improvised market place. He then glanced in the rearview mirror and caught his breath, unable even to utter the expletive that had formed in his brain.

Careening toward him was a massive truck, and it was on fire. It had lost its brakes and was barreling down the road toward the traffic jam like a flaming five-alarm bowling ball making to strike hundreds of frightened, immobile pins. Victor looked around desperately, but the traffic jam made it impossible to move his car. Just as he opened the door to throw himself out, the truck of fire veered off the road into the sand, which slowed it down before it rammed into a pile of hay and came to a complete stop. A strange quiet descended over the mass of people, cars, and fire, until a faint *click* broke it and the driver slowly emerged from the cab of the truck, grinning.

Soon everyone was grinning, even Victor, happy they had all escaped impending doom and had become instead an audience to a brilliant spectacle. They were so happy it took several minutes for them to remember they were in their cars trying to go somewhere. As that realization sunk in, many locals got out of their cars to help direct traffic, abandoning their own cars in the middle of road and requiring others to direct traffic around those cars.

At last, Victor made it home and collapsed, still in his dusty clothes, on his bed. His eyes were on the verge of closing when his phone rang. With his last ounce of energy, he clicked the phone on.

"I'm not here," Victor said.

"It's Lesotho National Day!" Zed yelled into the phone as though he were announcing Victor had just won a fabulous prize. "A favorite reception on the diplomatic circuit, mostly for the free drinks. Get your lazy ass up."

Victor fixed himself a double espresso and was out the door in a clean suit a few minutes later. He crossed the city's Independence Plaza and entered the Ajakar Sofitel, its brown and orange façade— likely considered modern and chic in colonial times when it was built—now passé and dull. He traipsed across the faded carpet and entered the main ballroom, grabbing a glass of wine from a passing waiter's tray. He took a cursory look around to see who was there, secretly hoping no targets of interest were in attendance so he could go back home.

In a corner he saw the ambassador from Iran, nibbling *hors d'oeuvres* and speaking respectfully to a crowd gathered around him. This was always awkward, Victor knew. His country and Iran had cut diplomatic ties back in 1980, yet diplomats from both countries often found themselves at the same receptions, delicately avoiding each other. It occurred to Victor that, with his native Italian, he could likely speak to the ambassador without him realizing Victor was, in fact, from the US Embassy. And it would be really fun to report the encounter to Zed tomorrow, just to see the *Oh shit!* look on his face. But he decided to let the opportunity pass.

He spotted a local businessman he knew, Enzo Maretti, an Italian descendant whose family had been in Pigallo enough generations that they now had Pigallese citizenship. Enzo's manners always allowed others to ease into a social scene, rather than dive head first into a crowd of strangers. Victor clapped his shoulder.

"Victor," Enzo said, genuinely pleased to see him. He opened some space for Victor in the circle of cheery, chattering guests. "You're just in time. We were making bets on next week's announcement of where the next World Cup will be held." Enzo turned to the others in the circle. "Victor is that rare thing, an American who likes football."

"Soccer," Victor corrected him. "And which country gets awarded the tournament will depend on who transfers the most cash to the right Swiss bank account." The other guests laughed, signaling their agreement by toasting each other, glasses clanging among the merriment.

"Be careful, Victor," Enzo said gaily. "I guess you haven't met Axl." Enzo motioned to one of the revelers in the circle.

"Axl Steiger," the man said, producing a business card that identified him as a vice president at Helvetica Bank in Zurich.

"So you know exactly what I'm talking about," Victor winked.

Axl smiled. "I'll neither confirm nor deny."

Victor judged Axl's suit as expensive but uninspired and determined the man himself to be rather ordinary but oddly needy.

The amusing chatter continued, and soon Axl excused himself to get another drink. Victor kept joking with Enzo and the others, then politely pulled himself away. A Swiss banker was a potential lead. For what, he wasn't sure. But it was worth taking some time to find out.

He circled the room a few times, nodding and smiling at other guests and occasionally saying hello to those he knew. He found Axl out on the balcony smoking.

"Mind if I join you?" Victor asked, pulling a pack of cigarettes out of his pocket.

"Not at all." Axl took out a lighter and lit Victor's cigarette.

Victor exhaled smoke as both men looked out over Independence Plaza. "How does a Swiss banker end up in Ajakar?"

"Only part Swiss," Axl corrected him. "I'm also German." He sipped his wine and stifled a yawn. "You'll have to forgive me. I only arrived this morning. I'm still in a bit of cloud. Yesterday at this time I was on a yacht off Ibiza." He took a long drag on his cigarette. "Do you know the Crown Prince of Ombudai?"

"Not personally," Victor said. "I once ate in a Georgetown restaurant with his son."

"You know his family then?"

"No, I mean I was in the restaurant at one table, and I recognized his son sitting at a different table with a few co-eds."

"The Crown Prince asked me to come look into a few investments in Pigallo for him."

"You were on his yacht in Ibiza?"

"Correct. Yesterday I was drinking pink champagne and eating caviar surrounded by women in thongs. Today I am surrounded by an unpleasant fish smell and drinking bad wine with you." He turned to Victor and smiled.

"In my defense," Victor said, "you've never seen me in a thong." Axl laughed and Victor continued, "It's not Ibiza, to be sure. But Ajakar has its charms. Have you visited the market?"

"It's true I could use more wooden hippo statues in my life, but I was hoping for something a little more interesting."

"Do you play golf? They have a decent golf course overlooking the ocean. If the wind is blowing the right direction, it doesn't even stink."

A door behind them opened. Victor turned to see a curvy woman sway toward them. She sparkled. She had diamonds in her ears and crystals on her dress and shoes. She latched herself on Axl's arm and began delicately biting his ear.

"I guess you didn't travel from Ibiza alone," Victor said.

"Olga, meet Victor." Olga took her tongue out of Axl's ear just long enough to acknowledge Victor with a pouty nod of her head. "Olga is a niece of the Crown Prince."

"Of course she is," Victor replied.

"I'd better get her upstairs. But golf sounds good. This weekend?"

"I'll set it up." Victor lit another cigarette as he watched Axl walk back inside with a shiny trophy on his arm. *A Swiss banker with expensive tastes and direct access to the Crown Prince of Ombudai,* Victor thought. *A good lead indeed.*

CHAPTER EIGHT
NUAKABATU, REPUBLIC OF ZUZU

Victor was once again standing under the cold hose drizzle in Nuakabatu's hotel bathtub. He'd had to cancel his golf game with Axl Steiger on short notice. He had reported the introduction to Director and Zed was enthusiastic about the possibilities, but when Abdul signaled an emergency meeting, Victor set Axl aside and jumped in the office car to head north. The drops of water were beginning to make a dent in the layer of sand on Victor's skin when he heard a low rumbling that seemed to be getting closer. He looked out the window.

"Holy shit!" He dove into the tub, curled up, and covered his head. He heard a loud explosion and felt the building shake beneath him. He grabbed his phone out of his pants piled on the bathroom floor and called Zed.

"There's a tank outside the hotel!"

"A tank? Hold up the phone."

Victor held up the phone. The tank rumbled some more.

"A T-90. Russian." Zed was perfectly calm.

"You can tell that just from the sound?"

"Stop shittin' your pants, monkey boy. Get your ass outside. Find out what the fuck is going on."

Victor pulled on some clothes and ran down the stairs to the street. Behind the tank were lines of Toyota pickup trucks with guns affixed to their roofs. Row upon row of men and boys were marching into the capital. They wore brightly colored fluffy wigs, and many had the glazed-over look of incessant qat chewers addicted to the root that kept them steadily high. They looked like a Bozo the Clown convention on crack.

The tank stopped and the soldiers halted behind it. For a moment, everything went quiet. Victor heard a clanging sound coming from inside the tank. He watched as the top unfolded. A handsome man wearing Ray-Ban Aviators and hoisting an AK-47 emerged.

"Zed, it's bin Fuqin."

"Go check on the ambo."

Victor ducked behind a building, cut through a dirt road, jumped over a goat, and made his way to the embassy. From outside the compound, he could see a figure on top of the roof—a man, hunched and grasping something to his chest. He was screaming, "Don't let them take my feta!" He ran from one side of the roof to the other, screaming about his feta cheese, and then a huge puff of white powder appeared above him. "*Please,* come and find me! *Someone!* I can't go through this again!" Another puff of white powder exploded.

Victor squinted at the crazed figure. Was Nash throwing *flour* on the roof? Victor could only assume he was expecting a rescue helicopter and was marking the roof so his rescuers could find him.

"Where are the Marines?" He threw another batch of flour up. "Can't you see me? Don't let them take me!"

Bin Fuqin's troops were several blocks away, and it was eerily quiet at the embassy. Victor yelled up to the roof. "Ambassador Nash? You need to come down. Your staff will need you to lead them through any evacuation."

The ambassador, covered in flour, glared down at Victor and thrust a long arm out at him. "*You!* You should have told me this was coming! What good are you guys if you can't see a coup coming?"

Victor threw his hands in the air and yelled back, "I did tell you! Now get back inside!"

"I'm writing you up as soon as I get out of here!"

A uniformed Marine appeared on the roof. The ambassador rushed to him and threw his arms around him, hugging the Marine close and falling to his knees.

***

The coup was over by the time Victor made it back to the hotel. Bin Fuqin had taken control of the radio and TV stations and secured the presidential palace without another shot being fired. Tata, according to the news, had spent the coup curled up under his desk crying. It was his wife and her twin sister—who was Tata's mistress—who had managed to secure the presidential plane and fly the family—along with several diamond necklaces, Tata's collection of leopard skins, and a faux Ming vase (made in China)—to Pigallo, where Pigallese President Wobuza had offered them asylum in return, it was reported, for a diamond necklace and one of the twin sisters.

At 3 p.m., bin Fuqin came over the airwaves to make a speech.

"My fellow Zuzuans, the autocracy has been abolished! The dictator Tata has fled! As a symbol of our newly won freedom and the establishment of rule by the people, I hereby decree that the Republic of Zuzu shall henceforth be called the Democratic Republic of Zuzu! Today shall be commemorated annually as the Feast of Triumph of Moral Righteousness over Wickedness, and every citizen will be required to slaughter a goat in honor of this great event!"

Victor clicked off the radio and made his way to his meeting point with Abdul. This time, he wore a straw hat he had picked up in the market.

"The Core is behind this," Abdul said to Victor. "They have an agreement with bin Fuqin. They're planning on using Zuzu as their staging ground. The Core is grooming Suqqit. They are promoting him to emir and sending him for training in Ombudai." He paused a moment and then said, "You know, Victor, one cannot remain an emir for long without proving his true worth."

"A hit on a western target?"

"It is expected of all emirs."

"Thanks, Abdul."

"Victor, one last thing." Abdul grabbed Victor's arm and looked him straight in the eye. "Get me out of here. They suspect me. I can make my way to Gabimbia. I'll be safe there, for a while. But you have to get me out soon. After everything I have given you and your government, you can do this for me."

They quickly devised a communication plan for meeting up in Gabimbia, a tiny country just south of Pigallo. Victor shook Abdul's hand and said, "I'll contact you in Gabimbia. You have my word."

***

Omar had spent the coup in the streets with his men, backing up bin Fuqin's soldiers and marching behind the general's tank.

His tunic was ripped and dirty and slightly marked up with makeup from some of bin Fuqin's younger fighters who had used the makeup for clown-like war paint. When the celebratory gunfire broke out to mark their victory, Omar decided to go back to his tent and avoid the inevitable rainfall of bullets that nearly always left someone on their own side injured.

He entered the tent and found Zawiki in a pristine *dishdasha,* slurping camel's milk out of a dirty cup and talking on the phone. He had clearly skipped out on the fighting.

"That's correct, sir. We have succeeded. And we certainly thank the Core for all your support." Zawiki was beaming as he listened to what Omar inferred was congratulatory praise. "I appreciate that. I certainly did work hard." He listened a moment then laughed out loud. "I'll do that! I will go have a piece of baklava! You take care now, and we'll see you soon!"

Omar returned to his quarters to shower and pack. He detested Zawiki's attempts to outmaneuver him, but he determined to set those frustrations aside for now. After all, he was now the Emir of the Core in the Desert.

CHAPTER NINE
AJAKAR, PIGALLO

By the time Victor made it back to Ajakar Station the following day, Zed had already written up the events in Nuakabatu and was bitching about the fact that he now had to deal with ex-President Tata and his coterie. They had firmly ensconced themselves in one of Wobuza's guesthouses while Wobuza begged the CYA for more money to help pay for the hospitality that such a dedicated ally in the TWOT deserved. "The guy's just been overthrown and he's asking his host for monogrammed sheets?" Zed complained.

Victor sat down in his chair to write up what he had learned from Abdul and to request permission to get Abdul out of Gabimbia, but nearly fell over when the back of the chair wobbled out of place. He realized he could barely see over his desk because the chair was so low, and the desk, which used to be wood, was now a dark gray metal. He tried to pump his chair up higher but there was no lever under the seat. As Victor was taking in these changes, Joseph the Support Officer entered the shark tank and winked at

Victor while pretending his index fingers and thumbs were guns he was shooting.

"I finally got the office furniture for your pay grade," Joseph said. "Had it shipped over from Virginia."

Victor looked across the room and saw his old GS-15 furniture sitting unused against a wall.

"Good thinking, Joseph," Victor said.

"You're welcome," said Joseph. He began counting staples.

Victor propped his elbows up on the desk, which was at the level of his chin, and started typing.

CHAPTER TEN
AJAKAR, PIGALLO

Victor was restless. He had devised a simple exfiltration plan for Abdul and despised having to wait for permission from Director to move ahead. He knocked on Zed's door.

"Enter," Zed said. He finished reading a cable on his computer screen before turning to Victor. "Seems the IÜD, in its race to reduce redundancies to help us cooperate, hired too many people. The office has 'overachieved' its objectives and now has an 'overstrength' issue."

"Maybe they'll form a new committee to examine the committee that was supposed to reduce redundancies."

"It's a good idea," Zed agreed. "Why did you come in here?"

"I haven't gotten a response on the request to exfiltrate Abdul. The guy's a proven asset whose info has been corroborated time and again, and Director is content to let the guy sweat it out in Gabimbia."

Zed glanced at a calendar on his wall. "It's gingerbread house competition time. An annual event. Director's minions are all sculpting Leesburg-style duplexes out of cookies. Who's got time to answer an exfiltration request?"

"Are you serious? John Boy can't find a minute to get the permission?" Victor asked, referring to the trainee who handled all the cables from Ajakar.

"John Boy is one of the finest gingerbread house builders. Director gave him a gift certificate for the Cheesecake Factory for his efforts last year."

Victor threw his hands out as if trying to wash away the conversation. "Can I at least call the FBI up here on this Suqqit thing? Maybe we can coordinate our efforts out here so his movements don't fall between the cracks back in Washington?"

"Who the fuck's got time to meet with the FBI? Director's breathing down my neck for a cable to the IÜD about what we're doing here at station to work closely with other agencies. I don't have time for a fucking meeting."

"Thanks, chief." Victor returned to his work area. He had found some phone books to stack on his chair so he was at the right height when sitting at his new desk. He sat down just in time to hear a beep from his computer. He looked over.

HABIBI: Ciao, bello.

Victor's instant message window had popped up. Habibi. He and Victor had been in training together, and he had served in Pigallo just before Victor. Despite his efforts never to be promoted, he was now a manager for Director.

HABIBI: Rumor is Nash wants your head.

VICTOR: Why? I told him the coup was coming.

HABIBI: Exactly, fuckwit. You told him the truth. Next time tell him what he wants to hear, so when the shit goes down he's got someone else to blame.

VICTOR: Excellent advice. How's Director?

HABIBI: The coffee is great. Ever since they put a Starbucks in. Anyway, I'm outta here. I volunteered to go to Rubblestan. I need a rest.

VICTOR: You realize how that sounds? You're going to the war zone because you need a rest...

HABIBI: The commute here is fucking killing me. And I'm stuck here reading cables all day. That's all I do. Fourteen hours a day. I read cables. Which is hard for me, you know. My English is not so good.

VICTOR: At least you can put your native Pashtu to good use in the badlands.

HABIBI: Nope. I'll be managing someone else who will be working with the locals.

VICTOR: Does he speak Pashtu?

HABIBI: Korean.

"Caro!" Zed yelled from across the office. "Grace me with your presence!"

Victor stood up and a phone book tumbled from his chair to the floor with a thud. He kicked it under his desk and walked to Zed's doorway. Zed looked at him expectantly, as though Victor ought to know why his chief had called him in. When Victor stared back blankly, Zed finally blinked, screwing up his face in annoyance.

"You didn't read it? Do you ever read cables?"

"We get thousands of cables a day. I can't read them all," Victor said.

"Can you read the ones about your cases?"

Victor shrugged.

"Director is *concerned* with your development of Axl Steiger," Zed said. He made air quotes as he said the word "concerned." "Legal got word of it. We can't recruit Swiss nationals. Some bullshit about neutrality."

"He's also German."

"Right, so Director wants you to assess his level of Swissness. To determine whether or not you can recruit him."

"Did they actually use the word Swissness?"

"Yes."

"How does one determine how Swiss a person is?"

"Fuck if I know. Start a fight with someone. See if he takes sides."

"You and I both know the Crown Prince finances terrorism. He was the main financier of the attacks on the United States. Steiger can give us the goods."

"If he can give us the goods wearing lederhosen, fine. If he shows up carrying a Swiss Army knife, the case is over. Figure it out."

***

Victor was still trying to remember the combination for his file safe a few days later when Zed's voice boomed across the office.

"Caro! Get your ass in here!"

Victor hurried out of the shark tank to Zed's office.

"Chief?"

"The sages at Director have surmised that, given his relocation to Gabimbia, Source Abdul is no longer of any use to us and we should terminate the relationship. Go to Director. See if you can get their head out of their ass."

CHAPTER ELEVEN
WASHINGTON, DC

The parking lot stretched endlessly in all directions, like an asphalt ocean with waves of cars. Victor wound his way through row after row looking for an open space. The lot was always full, now that Director had hired so many new employees as part of the IÜD's campaign to reduce redundancies. Director wanted to add a new parking lot, but feared reprisals from the powerful neighborhood association of the wealthy housing subdivision next door, whose members included an ex-vice president who would sit like a curmudgeon at the local Starbucks down the street.

Finally, Victor found a free parking space and began the ten-minute trudge to get to the building that housed Director. It was one-half glass cube, one-half brick cube, each with exactly the same internal layout. It was an architect's way of bringing an old concept into modern times while staying true to Director's nature: seemingly more transparent but with little change to the foundation.

Victor swiped his badge and entered another world: a twenty-four-hour, caffeine-infused bureaucratic ecosystem bubbling with the energy of countless nameless faces rushing about looking busy.

The world's highest-revenue Starbucks was packed, and the ordering line snaked down the main corridor and around the corner. A woman wearing three-inch heels was plodding down the hall with all the grace of an animatronic T-Rex. A young man with an ugly tie that was tied too short rammed Victor's shoulder as he hurried past, his rubber-soled shoes squeaking as he went. Victor passed a sign outside the cafeteria that advertised Chinese cooking classes every day next week from noon until two.

He turned down the side corridor that led to the Counterterrorism Department. Photographs from Rubblestan lined the walls. Victor stopped to study a photo of a group of elders who had gathered for a tribal meeting. They looked stately as they stared into the camera, noticeably aware of their burden to find a lasting solution for peace. Victor looked closer at each wise, worn face. One elder in the back row had his index finger shoved all the way up his nose. Victor studied the tableau and decided the photograph was symbolic of the entire war: so much solemnity broken by a tiny fit of ridiculousness. He turned and walked on.

Inside the department, lines of cubicles housed the Electronic Paper Pushers, known by their acronym, EPPs. The sharp rise in hiring over the last year had led to the installation of more and smaller cubicles, so that one room, which used to be a private office, now contained eight EPP stalls along either wall. Victor thought the EPPs looked like cows in their stalls waiting to be milked. He wondered when Director would start stacking cubicles in the drive to reduce redundancies.

As Victor walked through, a young woman leaned back in her chair and cried out, "Victor!" It was a call of salutation, but Victor thought he also heard desperation. With her pale face, eyes sunken into deep dark circles, and her cheeks so emaciated that her cheekbones looked like knives, Victor hardly recognized Jenna. She had been top in her class at Harvard and came to fight the good fight after the attacks. Now, she was so pale it was hard to see her against the non-descript beige of her EPP partition.

"Victor, it's so good to see you."

"Hey, Jenna. Looks like Director's keeping you busy."

"I work a lot, it's true. But we have to, given the state of the world and all those threats. Every day, more threats come in. There's just so much to do."

"What do they have you doing?"

"I'm working on Director's anti-inconsistency uniformity program. It's part of how Director is contributing to the IÜD's pro-active augmentation of systemization of the intelligence community."

"That sounds complicated," Victor said.

"Someone emails me a report. I email it to someone else, who emails it to someone else. Then eventually it comes back to me with suggestions for deleting a comma or adding a hyphen."

Suddenly, a voice sang from a loud speaker, "It's eleven a.m. Everyone up!" The EPPs jumped up in unison. "Arms way up to the ceiling!" the voice said with gusto. The EPPs obeyed, reaching up. "And down to your toes!" They all reached down.

"What the fuck is this?" Victor asked Jenna.

She giggled and bent into a yoga tree pose. "A few months ago, Director introduced the Krispy Kreme Kart," she said, speaking over the singing voice instructing everyone to bend and stretch. "It was meant as a morale booster. The Kart brought Krispy Kreme donuts to people at their desks. But then the medical unit started noticing that employees were getting fatter. I mean, donuts delivered to your desk? People just stopped moving. So then Director OK'd paid workout time, hoping employees would go exercise a bit, without it even counting as their lunch hour. But it didn't take. It's just too easy to sit at your desk and eat donuts. So then Director introduced five minutes of mandatory exercise every day at eleven. So here we are." She reached up to the ceiling with flared hands.

Victor left Jenna to her exercise and headed over to the section that handled West Africa and the Brotherhood. It was deserted, except for a secretary sitting at a reception desk. She wore a *boubou,* the bright flowing robes and headscarf that are the traditional dress in West Africa. Victor figured this was her way of showing solidarity with the culture she had experienced once for two days on a work visit to Pigallo.

Victor passed a conference room where it seemed the section's entire EPP pool was eating donuts. He continued, wending through the empty EPP stalls until he heard the clicking of a keyboard in a far-off corner. He followed the sound, hopeful that at least one person was working. He peeked over the EPP stall to see John Boy, engrossed in his work and typing furiously.

"Hey, John Boy. You're not at the meeting?"

"Hey, Victor." John Boy glanced back at the conference room where everyone was eating donuts. "I'm not important enough for that meeting. Management is meeting to decide when to hold an office-wide meeting to discuss a weekly meeting schedule."

"That's a lot of meeting. What are you working on?"

John Boy's face lit up. "I'm really onto something here. Look at this." He turned his monitor and Victor saw a complex link chart, a spider web of information. "I think I've discovered a new terrorist organization. It's amazing we didn't see it before. It started as a simple name search, but then the names just kept repeating and repeating, and then it hit me. These guys are all related! And they're *everywhere!* They've got a presence on every continent, every country! It's incredible, the tentacles on this monster."

"Who are they?"

"The FNU LNUs. This is serious, Victor. I'm putting together a package for Director right now. This is going straight to the top."

"Good job, John Boy." Victor patted him on the back. "I think I'll go get some coffee before my meeting."

He stifled a laugh as he made his way back to the main corridor. He appreciated John Boy's enthusiasm, how he threw himself fully into a project. Victor kind of even missed the days when he had been so enthusiastic. But at one point, Victor knew, someone would have to explain to John Boy that FNU LNU was an acronym meaning First Name Unknown, Last Name Unknown, used in a database to describe someone whose only crime was remaining nameless to Director. John Boy was linking random unknown people together into the world's newest menace.

Victor arrived at Starbucks and got in line.

"Hey, Victor!"

Victor scanned the café and saw his friend Jacob slouched on one of the couches.

"Hey, Jacob! How the hell are you?" Victor took his espresso and joined Jacob, a tall, good looking blond who, like Habibi, had been in training with Victor. The three of them had raised hell at the training center. When they had each received a laptop, Victor promptly made his startup sound the Iraqi national anthem, Habibi made the Iranian flag his screen saver, and Jacob had downloaded

London club music that he would blare at eleven o'clock at night when they were too exhausted to finish their cables.

Unlike Habibi and Victor, though, Jacob was a deep cover officer, meaning he worked without the luxury of diplomatic immunity, posing instead as a businessman. While most spies were considered to be out in the cold, deep cover officers were more like residents of Siberia. They operated without a safety net of any kind.

For a long time, Jacob had gotten a kick out of this kind of lifestyle. He traveled far and often and had been honored with a golden plaque marking his own private resting room in the international terminal in Tokyo. This kind of thing invigorated him. And he was good, really good, at manipulating people and leaving them thinking they were in total control. He could sell shit to Mr. Clean and have Mr. Clean placing an order for six months' inventory. But now Victor thought Jacob looked deflated.

"I can't do it anymore, Victor," Jacob said, motioning to the sitting area of Starbucks and the corridors beyond. "I don't like managers. I don't like trainees. I don't like case officers. I don't like the cleaning woman in my office. I don't like donuts. I don't like anyone who works for this agency. Or other agencies. I don't like anyone who works for government. Or in the public arena in general." He turned and looked Victor in the eye. "Maybe Washington, DC, isn't the right place for me."

"You think?"

"You know what happened to me yesterday? I was asked to trace a name. I got no hits. None. We had no record of the guy whatsoever. Then, I punch the guy's name into Google. *Google,* for Christ's sake. First hit I get says the guy is a terrorist. *First fucking hit.* But us? *Nothing.*"

"Have you seriously thought about leaving?"

"I can't. I'm screwed. My company, the one everyone *thinks* I work for, is under investigation for fraud."

"Oh shit."

"How is that gonna look on my resume? Ten years working in the derivatives division of a major hedge fund that's just gone down as a Ponzi scheme. Yeah, I'm totally employable."

"What are you going to do?"

"I don't know. I sit way in the back of my office in an EPP stall where I thought no one would find me. The more I ignore people, the more they come visit me. The less work I do, the friendlier my supervisor is. And he always asks me about my kids. Only, I don't have any kids. Then this morning, he tried to give me a fist bump. He just stood there, fist out, waiting."

"What'd you do?"

"Came to Starbucks. What else?"

***

Victor took his coffee with him back to the Counterterrorism Department for the meeting about Source Abdul. The furniture in the conference room had not been replaced since 1972, but new video conferencing equipment lined one wall. Victor double checked the room number then looked back at the conference table, where a group of twenty-somethings were discussing the new Halo 3 video game and its clear symbolic parallels to the Total War on Terror.

"I mean, they live in *caves,* you know," said one young woman, who was wearing a tank top and flapping a flip-flop against her heel, making a loud slapping sound. Her nose and left eyebrow were pierced, and a butterfly tattoo was clearly visible on her left shoulder. "And they have to, like, rely on asymmetrical warfare to, like, overcome the overlord."

"That's just it. Don't they see the overlord only wants to, like, help?" said a Justin Bieber lookalike.

"The overlord bombs their villages! Don't you see? Of course they fight back."

John Boy brushed past Victor. "Enough Halo, guys. Do you all know Victor?"

It was then that Victor realized, with a slight unease, that John Boy—who was planning to convince Director that a group of thugs with no names was about to take over and destroy the world—was going to run this meeting. The fate of Abdul rested with a group of tweens.

Victor, nervous and apprehensive, sat down at the table just as the young tattooed woman popped a large, pink bubblegum bubble in her mouth with a short, clear *snap!*

"Victor, we've gone over Abdul's case profile," John Boy said. "We appreciate the work he's done for us in the past. But let's face it, if he's in Gabimbia, he can't give us information on Zuzu. He's just no use to us anymore."

"I've never been to Gabimbia," one of the tweens chimed in. "But this one time, I went to Costa Rica. I stayed in this great hostel. Me and my friends went zip lining." All the tweens turned to her with wide, expectant eyes. Victor couldn't believe it. They actually looked *interested*. He jumped in before she could continue to steer the meeting off topic.

"If he goes back to Zuzu, bin Fuqin will kill him and his family."

"We can provide some information on life insurance policies," John Boy said.

"Abdul has been a good source, a great source, for more than a decade. He's the one who warned us about Tata's plans to nationalize the peanut industry months before it actually happened. When the Brotherhood started laundering peanut money through diamonds, that was Abdul who told us. He's put his life on the line for us, and why? For a few thousand dollars a year? No. Because he believes we are the good guys. He believes good still exists in this world, and that *we* are that good."

Victor heard a whirring sound coming down the hallway toward the conference room. A large woman in a Pepto-pink tent dress and sneakers rode into the room on a motorized cart. A wire basket was perched on front, nearly overflowing with papers. On the side was an oversized cup holder in which sat a gallon-sized sippy cup with the Diet Dr. Pepper logo splashed on it. This was Peggy, one of Director's managers who was now involved in the IÜD's community-wide TWOT efforts.

"Sorry I'm late. I was in a meeting with our liaison to the representative to the undersecretary to the deputy of Congressional Affairs. This Abdul thing has taken on a new life."

Victor saw that she had taped a photograph of herself holding three dogs to the front of the basket on her cart.

"Congress has informed the IÜD and Director that we are not meeting our financial objectives," Peggy continued. "It seems some members of Congress are not pleased with our financial dispensary rate."

"Now we can't get Abdul out because it will be too expensive?" Victor asked, incredulous.

"Just the opposite," she said, turning to him. "Congress doesn't think we're spending enough money fast enough. It makes us look like we're weak on terrorism. They want this to be the most expensive exfiltration operation we've ever seen. And you have to work with the Pentagon, Special Forces. A lot of emphasis on cross-agency cooperation. We have to demonstrate that we are working jointly with other groups in the government."

"I don't really need that much," Victor said. "A small plane and a pilot, and some cash to help him start a new life. Once he's out of the region, he's safe. With a new identity, he can go wherever he wants to go."

"That just won't do, Victor. I've just budgeted fifteen million dollars for this operation, to prove to Congress we're spending the money they're giving us efficiently and to send a message that we are strong on national security and willing to work with our partners in other agencies. You've now got a plane, a helicopter, two tanks, and twenty men at your disposal. Good luck, and thank Abdul for us for all his hard work." Peggy whirred her cart around and left the room.

"I totally need more caffeine," said the girl in the tank top. "Who wants to go to Starbucks?"

The tweens got up and left. Victor sat staring at the wall.

CHAPTER TWELVE
OMBUDAI

A loud drum awoke Omar and the other Core members in the nearby tents. The sun was just rising above the horizon, turning the sand into ripples of brilliant yellow, as Omar stepped out of his tent and breathed in the heavy morning air of Ombudai's desert. He smiled. Today was the first day of emir training.

Under the shade of an acacia tree, the mentor, a member of Core Central Leadership from Rubblestan, welcomed the emirs-to-be, who came from many of the other Core franchises, including the Core in the Peninsula and the Core in the Islands. Like Omar, they were hardened fighters with years of experience and a dream of striking the West.

"You are all integral members of this team," the mentor began. He wore a thick turban and a patch over one eye. His right hand grasped an AK-47, which he swung around wildly, as the mentor tended to talk with his hands. "Only by working together can we reach our destination, through the expansion of jihad across the globe. That is our mission. That is why we are all here. And this week, God willing, I shall impart to you the wisdom that is necessary to achieve our objective." The mentor surveyed his students, looking from one to the next before speaking again in his clear, high-pitched voice. "Jihad never rests. It is for this reason that throughout this week, you shall fast from sun up to sun down. This is to prepare you if we ever must continue the struggle through our holy days of fasting and to plant a seed of strength in you should you ever need to engage in a hunger strike."

Omar's stomach gurgled. It was one of the hottest seasons in the Ombudai desert, and the days were long.

"By the end of this week, each of you shall have developed a plan to strike a western target. Ascendancy to emir is impossible without it. Today, we begin with the essence of leadership: how to lead our fighters. Who can share an example of leadership, maybe a time you acted as a leader or someone around you showed good leadership?"

The rising Emir of the Core in the Kingdom spoke up. He was tall and had a thick mustache. "We were having a terrible time filling our number three slot," he said. Everyone murmured their immediate understanding of the problem. The Great Enemy had faced difficulties terminating those holding the top two posts in many Core franchises, but holders of the third post were routinely meeting their destiny through Hellfire missiles. "Nobody wanted the job. I offered it to several of my lieutenants. They all declined. I knew I needed a new perspective to attract the right fighter, so that position might be filled and our struggle could move forward. I stopped mentioning the great responsibilities of the position, and instead focused on the urgency to attain Paradise and its non-earthly delights, along with the fact that, if he didn't like the job, it was likely a short-term position." He smiled. "I have managed to fill that number three slot several times now."

The others acknowledged the brilliance of the new Emir of the Core in the Kingdom, murmuring their agreement and nodding their heads.

"Do you remember the car bomb attempt in the square named Times, in the village of New York?" Omar and the other men turned their attention to the Emir of the Core in the Peninsula. His beige robe had sweat stains down the front and beads of perspiration clung to his temples. "The car only smoked. It never blew up. And my follower, he left the keys in the trunk lock. Not just the car key, but all the keys, including those to the apartment where the plan had been formulated and the bomb had been built." Omar and the others groaned, lamenting what they agreed must have been a terrible setback. "There is a positive side to everything, though!" the emir from the Peninsula continued. He raised an index finger for emphasis. "The square named Times remains a valid target, and we shall focus on that good news."

"Do we have any other examples?" the mentor asked.

The Emir of the Core in the Islands raised his hand. "Our main bomb maker blew off both his hands." The others responded with various *oof!* and *ouch!* sounds. "I didn't know how to respond. I panicked. What do you do with a bomb maker with no hands? Is he not still a brother? And then the solution came to me." He paused. The others seemed to stop breathing in anticipation of his next words. "I placed him in our number three position." The emirs exalted in his creativity.

The conversation flowed under the acacia tree, and by the afternoon, the group had moved on to a discussion about using social media to control the message of each Core franchise and to recruit new adherents. Omar basked in the idea of using western technology against the West, an irony he had come to relish each time he picked up the American-made Stinger missiles he had acquired while fighting in Rubblestan.

"I did a full interview with *The New York Times* over Twitter," recounted the Emir of the Core in the Horn of Africa. "It allowed for some really nice back and forth. But Twitter recently closed our account. They said we violated the terms of service when we tweeted our plans to assassinate our president. We thought it was a great propaganda tool, but in the end we just looked silly. It's a blessing and a curse, Twitter."

By sundown the future emirs were exhausted and they idled on carpets in the main tent chewing qat and relaxing before going to bed.

"What do we start with tomorrow?" one of the emirs asked to the room.

"I think we're doing proper vest fitting," someone responded.

"That's in the afternoon," said another. "I think we start with a discussion on body shaving. Do you brothers have trouble with razor burn?"

"When is the falconry session?" asked yet another.

"I'm hoping to skip that one," Omar said. "We don't have falcons in Zuzu. We've done just fine using pigeons to carry our messages."

"Sorry, brother," one of the men said as he approached the carpet where Omar was in repose. "Core Central Leadership wants all emirs to be falcon certified. I was at the meeting in Rubblestan." He sat down next to Omar and put out his hand. "Akim," he said by way of introduction. His robe was freshly pressed and his sandals looked new. "Falcons have a better success rate. They are four times more likely to reach the intended message recipient than pigeons. Core Central did a study."

"You are based in Rubblestan?"

"The next Emir of the Rubblestan Central Brigade," Akim said with a little bow. "If I make it through this week. Don't tell anyone, but I snuck a few dates earlier during our break." He patted his stomach and winked at Omar. They both chewed their qat in silence for a minute. "Have you thought about your attack?" Akim asked Omar. "We've got a number of international forces in our area. I'm thinking a coordinated strike on some command centers, maybe an embassy or two. You?"

Omar mashed some of the qat leaves around in his mouth. "The United States."

"An embassy? A consulate? Maybe pick up some tourists?"

"No," Omar said looking at Akim. "*The* United States. An attack *inside*."

Akim let out a laugh that showed he was impressed. He shook his head in disbelief but kept smiling at Omar. "That's bold, brother. That's bold." He clapped Omar on the back and the two regaled each other in a qat-infused discourse over the myriad possibilities.

CHAPTER THIRTEEN
WASHINGTON, DC

Victor was still in shock as he walked back out to the main corridor. Abdul just needed a ride out of town and maybe a few thousand dollars to buy a car, rent a house, and start his life again. Victor started contemplating how to introduce tanks, helicopters, and burly men with unkempt ponytails and beards who would be looking for the same adrenaline rush they got on their last tour in Rubblestan into his new exfiltration plan. He walked past Starbucks, pushing through the late morning line that blocked the entire hallway, and gave a few waves and nods to colleagues he knew but whose names he had forgotten. He entered the quiet calm of the library to check his emails and reflect on his next move.

He scanned the subject lines of the emails. *"Tank usage in exfil ops," "New regulations on pets at work," "Get your ass back here!"* — that last one was clearly from Zed. One email in particular caught his eye. *"Congratulations, Victor." What was this?* He opened it and immediately cursed when he saw the form letter.

"Congratulations, Victor. The Office of Security has determined it is time once again for you to take the polygraph test. The polygraph test is an instrumental tool in maintaining the integrity of the CYA and is here to ensure your safety and that of your colleagues and the organization. We look forward to seeing you at the time designated below."

"Ah, fuck!" Victor said, logging off. To get over the bad news, he went to Starbucks.

***

Victor had once heard a former American diplomat refer to the polygraph as a "mental colonoscopy." However, with a colonoscopy, Victor guessed, the pain ended after about one hour and a nurse handed you a donut pillow on your way out the door. Victor's first poly was ten years ago and had lasted three full days. Still, on that third day, as he left the stuffy room covered in sweat and aching from being strapped to a chair for twenty-four of the previous seventy-two hours, he had not passed.

He had told them about his Basque girlfriend during college, after which they accused him of participating in subversive activities against an ally, Spain. He had told them how he had climbed the Brooklyn Bridge, after his interrogator insisted Victor had shown a reaction when asked if he had ever committed a felony. "It seemed like a great activity to do at two in the morning during senior week," Victor explained, wondering if he could get in retroactive trouble for every bad decision he had ever made.

At the end of those three days, he had failed to pass, but he had also failed to fail, and was thus granted his clearances. But he had learned the final lesson of the poly: Everything he had ever done in his life had been wrong, according to the CYA.

His second poly, five years later, had gone much better. It had lasted a relatively short two full days and Victor was accused of treason only twice.

This time, a man named Jim ushered Victor into a small room and motioned for him to sit in what looked like a cushioned electric chair adjacent to a desk. Up in a corner of the room was a thinly disguised camera, and on the wall behind the desk was a one-way mirror. Victor imagined a supervisor back there with a bucket of popcorn, waiting for the show to begin.

Jim began strapping Victor in. "I want you to know I'm here to help you." He fastened a cable around Victor's chest to monitor his heart rate and breathing. "If you just tell the truth, you'll be out of here in thirty minutes." He tightened a blood pressure band around Victor's arm. "My goal is to help you get through this as painlessly as possible." He stuck electrodes on both of Victor's temples and snapped a band around his head to hold them in place. "Just tell the truth. You'll be out of here in no time. Now, is there anything you want to tell me before we begin?"

Victor had decided to get things out in the open sooner rather than later this time around. Trying to look as serious as he could while wearing a bandage strapped around his head, he leaned forward to speak. The cables tugged, and he was forced to sit back again. "Why, yes, Jim. There is something I want to tell you before we begin." Victor adjusted the cable around his chest. "I think you're a fucking asshole and I don't know how you can look at yourself in the mirror every day. We're going to spend the next eight hours in this stuffy as shit room, and maybe even the next three days, with you implying I've done something wrong. Well, fuck you, you cubicle-dwelling gopher who's never left Northern Virginia but thinks he can tell me how to do my job. Your only job is to find a rat, and your next promotion depends on it. But you know what? You guys suck at it. Aldrich Ames passed his poly. Good work on that one. And now you're going to give me hell for actually doing my job. I don't sell secrets. I don't fuck chickens. I don't break into houses and steal women's underwear. I don't drug and rape women and videotape it, or steal credit cards, or even steal bacon. But I'm the guy you're going to give a hard time. So fuck you. Now, let's start."

Jim stared blankly at Victor for a moment. Victor was smiling.

"You said if I was honest, I'd be out of here in thirty minutes," Victor said. "That's what I was aiming for. Did the machine show you how honest I was being?"

Jim cleared his throat and the circus began.

He sat behind the desk. Then he moved to sit in front of Victor. He grimaced. He went back behind the desk. He smiled. He sighed. He nodded. He shook his head. He sat in front of Victor again, this time with his seat raised a little higher so Victor had to look up at him. He rolled up his sleeves. He leaned forward and glared. He sat back and smiled. He left the room. The heat went up. He came back with his own cup of ice water.

Three hours on, they hadn't made much progress.

"Are you a spy?" Jim asked.

"Yes."

"What did you say?"

"I said, yes, I am a spy. Perhaps you want to reword the question, like, am I a spy for a country other than the United States?"

"Yes, good idea. Are you a spy for a country other than the United States?"

"No."

"Do you like pizza?"

"Yes."

"Have you ever sold secrets?"

"Yes."

"Can you explain?"

"In sixth grade, I promised Leyla Adams I would tell her a secret if she gave me a dollar."

"What was the secret?"

"I can't tell you."

"What if I give you a dollar?"

"No."

"Why not?"

"I don't sell secrets anymore."

On and on it went. The heat went up. The cables were tightened around Victor's chest, moved to his ankle, moved to his thigh, and then back to his chest. Jim exited the room, came back, and left again. Finally, he returned and told Victor he could go.

As Victor unstrapped himself and stretched out of a sitting position, he said to Jim, "Thanks. I've really enjoyed our time together, and that's the honest truth." He walked out and went straight to the happy hour at the bar next to his hotel.

CHAPTER FOURTEEN
WASHINGTON, DC

Victor arrived at the airport hung-over, exhausted, and still mentally drained from the brain raking he had suffered the day before. He couldn't wait to get as far away from Director as possible.

"Welcome to USA Air. What is your final destination today and may I see your passport?" A bubbly brunette gave him a broad smile.

He stepped up to the counter. "Good afternoon. Ajakar." He handed over his passport.

The airline employee typed away and then suddenly crinkled her nose, as if she had just smelled something rotten. She typed more and looked more concerned. "Sir, you don't have a return ticket."

"Excuse me?" Victor said, as politely as he could through his cottonmouth. "This trip is my return ticket. I live in Ajakar."

"I'm sorry. Your visa has expired. We can't let you board."

Victor pulled out his identification card from Pigallo's Ministry of Foreign Affairs, which identified him as a diplomat in that country. "Look at the passport. It's a diplomatic passport, and here's my foreign ministry card. Pigallo gives a visa for six months, just enough time to get the diplomatic ID. The Pigallese government accepts this ID as proof that I can live in the country."

"If you don't have a return ticket, we can't let you board. We can't just let you stay in another country illegally."

"This *is* my return ticket. And since when is USA Air in charge of homeland security for Pigallo? Don't you understand? I am a diplomat. I represent the government of the United States in Pigallo. I live in Pigallo."

"If you don't buy a return ticket, we cannot let you board."

"You've got to be fucking kidding me. Fine. You want to play it like that? I want a fully refundable one-way ticket from Ajakar to Washington, DC."

The employee perked up again and started typing. "For which day, sir?"

"Pick a day. How about two weeks from today?"

She typed some more and her smile returned.

"You realize I'm just going to cancel that ticket as soon as I get to Ajakar."

The employee handed Victor his boarding pass. "Enjoy your vacation!"

***

Victor stood in the long passenger security line watching the circus act, which was always a reaction to the last threat. The shoe-bomber gave rise to the slip-on shoe industry to make it easier to take shoes off and put them on at the security checkpoint. The diaper-bomber ushered in the era of the full body scanner, providing much email fodder anytime a fat person, ugly person, or totally hot person got photographed down to his or her skivvies.

At least Victor knew if he ever felt lonely he could always come to the airport to get felt up.

He watched two officers in blue by the scanning machines collecting air samples and feeding them into their computer. One officer suddenly looked alarmed and nearly shouted to his partner, "Anthrax!" People in the security line started to panic, pushing each other and screaming uncontrollably.

"Wait! Wait!" the second officer shouted over the chaos. "Give it a minute." The crowd fell silent, watching the two officers watching the screen while the computer ran diagnostics. "Not anthrax!" the second officer yelled triumphantly. "It's not anthrax! It's just a virulent strain of foot odor!" The crowd exhaled in unison, pleased they had a unique story to tell about their experience at airport security at the next cocktail party or water cooler gathering.

Victor stepped up to the X-ray machine and unloaded his laptop and single saline bottle into separate bins, and doffed his jacket and belt before walking through the metal detector. As he was putting all his clothes back on, another officer called him over. He was short and fat and had such underdeveloped shoulders he looked like a pear.

"Sir, I'm afraid this saline bottle exceeds the Transportation Security Agency's regulatory limits."

"It says on it 'TSA-approved,'" Victor told the officer. "I figured that meant it was approved by the TSA. Look, it even has a picture of an airplane on it."

"Why is it not in a polymerized containment receptacle?"

"I'm sorry, I don't know what that means."

"A plastic bag. Why is it not in a plastic bag?"

"I only have one thing."

"Having a single item does not exempt you from having to conform to the polymerized containment receptacle regulation as laid out in the TSA's travel security code."

"If the purpose of a plastic bag is to keep all liquids and gels together, then what is the point of a plastic bag for a single bottle? There's nothing to keep the bottle together with."

"Wait here," the officer said. He walked around the X-ray machine to the front of the security area. He returned a moment later with a plastic bag, placed the saline bottle in the plastic bag, and placed the plastic bag in Victor's backpack.

"That's quite a deterrent for a terrorist who wears contact lenses but hasn't invested in Ziploc bags," Victor said, smiling.

"That's exactly it, sir. We need to make it as difficult as possible for them. Enjoy your trip."

"Keep up the good work," Victor said.

CHAPTER FIFTEEN
AJAKAR, PIGALLO

Victor was hot but happy to be back in Ajakar. The familiar smell of rotten fish, burning garbage, and polluted ocean was comforting in its way, and it put a jaunt in his step as he walked to the office.

He surveyed the shark tank and saw no sign of Joseph the Support Officer, so he switched out his makeshift GS-13 chair with his old GS-15 one and leaned back in lumbar-supporting comfort. He picked up the phone to call his new best friend, Axl Steiger.

"I'm sorry we couldn't get that golf game in as planned," Victor said. He had never liked golf, but if that was his Swiss banker's favorite activity, it was now Victor's favorite activity, too. "Shall we try again this weekend?"

"That works great," Axl replied. "The Crown Prince's niece heads back to Ibiza, so I'll be ready for some bachelor time."

"It's a plan then. See you soon."

CHAPTER SIXTEEN
NUAKABATU, DEMOCRATIC REPUBLIC OF ZUZU

Omar found the heat of Nuakabatu refreshing as he stepped out of the stale air of the airplane after a long flight from Ombudai. He saw that in his short time away, the airport had been renamed Bin Fuqin International. Portraits of the new democratic leader lined the walls of the terminal: bin Fuqin in his finest military uniform; bin Fuqin surrounded by clouds and cherubic children; bin Fuqin looking serious in a Western-style suit and tie. Outside the terminal stood an enormous brass statue of bin Fuqin wrestling a lion to the ground.

While Omar found such idolatry distasteful, he figured it was a small price to pay for the freedom of movement the Brotherhood, freshly renamed the Core in the Desert, now enjoyed. He returned to his organization's base tent and quickly went about calling together his lieutenants. As he looked around the room, he noticed someone was missing.

"Where is Zawiki?" Omar asked. He knew that his leap to the front of the Core in the Desert had been troublesome for the ball-licking Zawiki, and he wanted to keep his ideological opponent as close as possible in order to prevent him from trying to implement any agenda of his own.

"You didn't hear?" said one of Omar's lieutenants. "He's been promoted. Core Central brought him to Rubblestan."

"Promoted?" Omar practically yelled. *How could Core Central allow this to happen?* This was the man who, for years, had failed to get the Brotherhood recognized, who had staged a series of failed rallies, and who had once smeared peanut butter on the wrong man's face in a case of mistaken identity.

"Actually, sir, we helped push the idea," said the lieutenant. "Zawiki was causing problems here. The troops didn't like him. We sent him to scout some sites in Europe while you were away. We gave him a fake passport with a fake name, but he used his real Hilton rewards card when he checked in so he could get the reward points. It was a real a setback. And he's pasty. Just a disgusting, pudgy, pastiness. Plus, he kept asking us to join him for a Turkish bath. We figured the best thing to do was to move him out. Make him someone else's problem."

"He also got moved up," said Omar.

"That was the downside. Surely they'll neutralize him in Rubblestan. They wouldn't give him any actual responsibility. Not when they see how full of air he is. I mean, he's really puffy."

Omar was not so sure, but he put Zawiki out of his mind, as he laid out his plan for the Core in the Desert's first spectacular attack.

CHAPTER SEVENTEEN
AJAKAR, PIGALLO

Victor and Axl sat under a large parasol at a table at the Ajakar Golf Club, overlooking the ocean. The sky was a clear baby blue and a light sea breeze tickled the air. The waiter came over to take their order. Victor signaled Axl to go first.

"The roast beef sandwich with a side of sauerkraut, please," Axl said, looking up from the menu. "Do you have anything other than Swiss cheese?"

As Axl and the waiter reviewed the cheese choices, Victor made a mental note of the order. *Sauerkraut is German, isn't it? And clearly the man doesn't like Swiss cheese. Would Director conclude that Axl has a low level of Swissness?*

Victor realized Axl and the waiter were staring at him, waiting for him to order. "Club sandwich, please." Victor put aside the Swissness question and focused his attention back on Axl, who was surveying the view as the waiter walked away.

"We're lucky," Victor said. "The wind is in the right direction. There's a fish market down below and the city's sewage comes out not far from here."

"They must pump the shit farther out."

"The plans called for a longer pipe, so the sewage would flow outside the bay. Not all the money made it to the project. The pipe had to be shortened. But you can see some really nice Mercedes being driven around town now."

"The realities of doing business in Pigallo, I suppose," Axl said and took a sip of his beer. "Luckily, the Crown Prince is well aware of such nuances. In fact, he rather enjoys investing in such gray areas. He recently purchased some real estate in the DRZ."

"The coup didn't scare him off?"

"On the contrary. He's been an active investor there. Mostly peanut distribution networks. But a lot of money." He drank some more beer. He glanced at Victor. "You'll keep that to yourself, right? I probably shouldn't be talking about my client's business interests."

Score! Little lights went off in Victor's head, like a pinball machine accumulating points. Phrases like "You'll keep that to yourself" and "I shouldn't be talking about this" were a case officer's wet dream. On the outside, he remained nonchalant. "Don't worry about it," he said, as though he had hardly taken notice of Axl's indiscretion. "Did you hear General bin Fuqin has taken a new name? The all-powerful and all-knowing great warrior of almighty stamina and virility and infinite courage who defeats all evil. You have to love a dictator with a name like that."

They toasted bin Fuqin and tucked in to their sandwiches.

***

Victor was pacing around the shark tank the following day, contemplating his next steps with Axl. He had reported the previous day's events and given his assessment to Director: Axl Steiger had great access and would be willing to talk.

"Stop. You're making me dizzy."

Victor snapped out of his reverie and saw Zed come in the shark tank. Zed pulled the GS-15 chair out of a corner and sat down. He fidgeted a bit then leaned back. "Comfy." He paused for a beat then looked straight at Victor. "Director wants you to cease contact with Steiger. It seems Legal doesn't consider sauerkraut a definitive litmus test of non-Swissness. Apparently the Swiss eat it, too. It was a good effort, though."

"What about his access?"

"Director was more concerned about the amount of time you're spending on the links." Victor was appalled. "Don't get all pissy. Director's appearing before the Senate Oversight Committee this week. Doesn't want to report that officers are playing golf instead of chasing terrorists. Your timing was off, that's all."

"That's bullshit."

"I know it's bullshit and you know it's bullshit. Director probably knows it, too. But I don't want any more cables about you trying to develop him."

"You're backing Director?"

"That's not what I said. I said *no more cables about you developing him.*" Zed let that sink in before walking out, leaving the comfortable office chair spinning.

***

Despite his setback regarding how Helvetian his banker friend was or was not, Victor needed to maintain his focus. Abdul was counting on him to get him to safety, and Victor prided himself on never letting down a source. On the lookout for Joseph, he took the comfortable chair from the middle of the office where Zed had left it and dragged it around to his desk to think.

Victor had been to Gabimbia once before, for that country's annual Air Force Air Show. The air show was a big event each year, even though Gabimbia's air force only had one plane, a small Rafale fighter jet that had been a gift from France five years ago. Given how small Gabimbia was, as soon as the airplane took off, it had to turn around immediately and land again, so as not to violate the airspace of its neighbors. Additionally, it could only take off on a north-south axis, because the country was not wide enough from east to west to allow the plane the necessary space to get airborne. But each year, Gabimbia's president gathered the region's diplomats for an air show, and the diplomats would applaud politely when the airplane took off and again when it landed five minutes later.

Victor had learned, after the air show and on his return trip to Pigallo from Gabimbia, that the national airline, Gabimbia Air, also had only one airplane. He had discovered this when he arrived at Gabimbia International Airport and was told that Gabimbia's first lady had decided to go shopping in Ajakar and had taken Gabimbia Air's one plane, which apparently also served as the presidential plane. Victor had sat in the terminal with the other passengers until the first lady had finished her shopping and decided to return home. Exhausted and sweaty, the passengers had all climbed aboard for the thirty-minute flight to Ajakar. Forty-five minutes later, they still had not landed. Victor had been about to ask a flight attendant why, when they began their descent. Victor had looked out the window to see not Ajakar, but Nuakabatu. When the plane landed, two men in business suits were standing on the tarmac waiting. The plane's door opened. The two men got on and hugged and shook hands with the pilot. They sat down in first class, and the plane took off again, finally to land in Ajakar. Inspired, Victor nearly ran to Zed's office. "They want the most expensive and elaborate exfiltration operation in the Agency's history? I've got it."

Zed swiveled away from his computer. "Sit."

Victor did. "First," he said. His eyes were big and bright and his hands accentuated his words. "We get a cargo plane."

"I like it already."

"I'll fly into Gabimbia under the cover of darkness and will instruct the pilot, who will believe he is providing routine transportation to a newly created aid organization—which will be fully backstopped with fabricated tax returns and a shop front in New Jersey—to land at the rendezvous point: a deserted field in the middle of Gabimbia."

"Next?"

"Upon landing at said rendezvous point, two tanks will exit the cargo plane and provide cover over the deserted field while I lead fifteen special operations forces officers out to gather Abdul and his baggage. A helicopter, which will launch from Pigallo's southern border with Gabimbia, will then penetrate Gabimbian air space and provide air cover while the special operations forces officers bundle Abdul into the waiting plane."

"That still leaves us with unused resources."

Victor continued, "The fifteen remaining special operations forces officers will deploy to the Gabimbian airport to neutralize that country's air force and ensure it makes no attempt to interfere in our exfil op. Once Abdul is safely in our custody, I will transport him to an undisclosed delivery point near the border axis of three Central African countries, providing him with triple egress access opportunities to move out of the region." Victor finally took a breath. "What do you think?"

"Director will love it. Type it up then get the fuck out of here to arrange the real plan."

CHAPTER EIGHTEEN
GABIMBIA

Victor entered Gabimbia's Ministry of Internal Security. The building was beige like the dirt around it and paint was curling off the walls. Victor gave a curt nod to the guard in front and walked to the door. The guard saluted and opened it for him. Victor passed the elevator, which had not worked for about thirteen years, ever since the building had begun to lean sideways and the elevator shaft was no longer aligned. He went into the stairwell.

Victor was covered in sweat when he reached the twelfth floor and walked into General Banja's office. In his crisp uniform, he stood to greet Victor and shook his hand with vigor. "Victor, my friend! Do come in! To what do I owe this honorable pleasure?"

"I've come to discuss a counterterrorism program I'd like to launch with you." Victor sat down and gave him the details.

***

The following week, two tanks, a cargo plane, a helicopter, and thirty special operations forces officers arrived in Gabimbia under Gabimbian military escort, which led them to a training barracks near the country's western frontier. General Banja rose to address his troops.

"Gentlemen, I am pleased to have you all here. Over the next forty-eight hours, you will participate in joint counterterrorism training exercises with your counterparts from the United States. We are grateful for their cooperation and are most pleased they are willing to help us secure our borders. They have generously offered nearly fifteen million dollars, excuse me, I mean fourteen million dollars for this training program." He glanced back for a second at a shiny Mercedes parked behind him and smiled.

As Banja spoke, Victor exited the barracks. Director would be placated, believing he had used all the necessary pieces of important equipment, personnel, and budget. With the Gabimbian security services fully ensconced in counterterrorism training, and with General Banja counting his nearly fifteen million dollars—minus the money Victor had taken out for Abdul and the $16.99 he had used to rent the battered Peugeot he was now driving—nobody would notice him while he made sure Abdul slipped out of the region.

Victor double-checked his backpack. He had one thousand dollars cash to give to Abdul, along with his new identity documents.

Abdul was waiting behind the country's only pizzeria, just as he and Victor had arranged, hoisting a large, braided plastic bag over his shoulder and holding a rope attached to a goat. When Victor stopped the car, Abdul opened the back door, threw his bag in, and helped the goat into the back seat before joining Victor in front. The goat sat quietly with his head peering through the opening between the two front seats.

"Here are your new documents," Victor said, handing him a passport and identity card. "I'll drive you to the airport just over the border in Pigallo. I've booked you on a flight tonight to Dar es Salaam, with an onward flight anywhere you want to go." Victor pulled out a stack of cash. The goat remained emotionless, but Victor could see Abdul was moved, eager to start a new life.

"Thank you, my friend. Thank you. Now, you take this." He handed Victor a thumb drive. "I have received information on al-Suqqit." He pointed to the thumb drive. "It's all there."

Victor, Abdul, and his goat drove toward the border and toward Abdul's new life.

CHAPTER NINETEEN
CALIPHATE CROSSING, RUBBLESTAN

The line of camels stretched out, row after row, until their beige fur blended in with the dirt where it met the horizon. Omar walked his camel down each row, growing more frustrated as he moved farther away from the entrance. He looked at the mountain, so distant now, and marveled at how it could host an entire cave complex inside. Caliphate Crossing, as Core Central headquarters had recently been named, looked to an outsider like any other mountain with hundreds of camels parked outside.

Omar found an open spot, carefully maneuvered his camel between two others, and tied the beast up.

He didn't like that Core Central had summoned him to Rubblestan. Up until now, he had been able to mount his attacks without prior approval. He had sought out Core sponsorship to help build his coffers and extend his reach beyond West Africa. He had not anticipated having to ask permission. Indeed, in advertising the opportunities to work with them, the Core expressly stated that they sought small terrorist groups that showed initiative and were willing to take risks. He feared that, in the rush to expand, these values were being lost.

Omar entered the cave complex and was overwhelmed by the energy and momentum that engulfed him. People were everywhere, moving this way and that, springing from nearly hidden cave corridors and disappearing down different ones. Around a bend he could hear loud chatting, which grew to a near roar as he got closer. He came around to find dozens and dozens of Core Central employees packed into a freshly built Teahadi café. The workers socialized while sipping chai.

Omar found corridor Q and turned down the fluorescent-lit tunnel that led to where his meeting was to be held. Along the cave walls were photographs depicting the Core's adventures overseas. Some showed the devastation—piles of rubble left after one of their successes—but most were of mid-level Core fighters scouting out places for new projects: warriors bundled up against the snow and freezing temperatures in Michigan; Core fighters enjoying Buffalo wings under a sign that read "Pluck U!" in Buffalo, New York; and others in fits of laughter after ordering a Rooty Tooty Fresh 'N Fruity breakfast at IHOP, although it was unclear which city they were in.

Omar continued to the conference cave and was taken aback when he entered. Sitting like an over-stuffed potato at the head of a group of barefoot men on a rug was Zawiki.

"Come in, Omar, and take a seat." Zawiki gestured to a cushion on the floor next to him and took a sip of his mint tea before grabbing a piece of yellow cake and shoving it whole in his mouth. "Good to see you." Crumbs fell out of Zawiki's mouth and onto his beard as he spoke.

"The men in Zuzu told me you had been transferred here. I trust you're enjoying your new position with Core Central."

"Have you seen the cafeteria? Who wouldn't enjoy it?" He licked a finger and used it to pick up the crumbs left on his cake plate. "But we didn't bring you here to talk about food. We figured we would use this opportunity to discuss your plans for your upcoming attack and to bring to your attention some changes that have been made here at Core Central headquarters."

Omar lamented that he had to sit there and listen to Zawiki, a man who had moved from cave cubicle to cave cubicle, but had not once planned, organized, or carried out an attack. Plus, Omar couldn't help but think of the goat ball incident.

"First of all," Zawiki began, while fiddling with his bare, bulbous toes that stuck out like dirty balloons from his sandals, "Core Central is now exercising increased control over the management of global jihad. Like the Core in the Desert, many other groups have sworn their loyalty to the Core and franchised the brand in their respective regions. Each has its own agenda, but there are many overlaps and redundancies. I'll give you an example." He used the hand that he had just been using to pick at his toes to wipe some spittle off his mouth. "We tasked a committee here at Caliphate Crossing with investigating what plans different Core franchises were developing. Do you know what the committee found? Not one, but three—*three!*—different groups were plotting to bring down the Eiffel Tower. That is a waste of time, money, and manpower. We found similar redundancies in London and Berlin. From now on, Core Central will be charged with streamlining and coordinating efforts like these."

Omar did not like where this was going but said nothing.

Zawiki continued, "Core Central will serve to transcend any differences Core franchises may encounter with one another and will ensure that what is in conflict shall be made harmonious. As we say, jihad is a communal effort. Now, in terms of your proposal, Omar, Core Central must insist you focus your efforts on the southeastern part of the United States. We recently had a group picked up in Buffalo, New York. Maybe you saw their picture on the way in? The Northeast is too sensitive right now. Core Central Leadership has other plans for the western part. Next," Zawiki looked down at his notes. "I understand your plot will involve noxious gases, is that right?"

Omar nodded.

"Great. But before we can release the funding for such a project, you're going to have to complete an online course about hazardous materials. We want to make sure Core warriors know how to properly handle these materials. We've recently had a few unfortunate incidents, which I won't go into. Suffice it to say, we won't be using the cafeteria for research again anytime soon. Excuse me a moment." Zawiki turned to a lieutenant who had just entered. "Yes?"

"Sorry to disturb you, sir. The Core in the Peninsula are asking if they can get business class seats for Operation Candlewax."

"I thought I handled this yesterday," Zawiki said, annoyed.

"They are insisting it's a really long flight and they need their wits about them."

"That plan calls for blowing up the plane after only eight hours!" Zawiki said. "Business class is only if they plan to blow it up after more than fourteen hours. I understand it might be uncomfortable, but a trip to Paradise doesn't come with first class seats." The lieutenant nodded at Zawiki and left.

"My apologies," Zawiki said to Omar. "Once you've completed the course, your plan will have to be approved by all the departments involved." Zawiki looked down at his notes again. "Based on what you want to do, you're going to need signatures from our Western Hemisphere Department, since the attack will take place in the United States. Within that department, you'll need a signature from each office that covers each city where you plan to hit a target. Then you'll need approval from our Conventional Explosives Unit, since you'll be blowing up the targets using C-4. Truck rentals will have to go through Transport and Logistics. The Weapons of Mass Destruction Group has to sign off on it, since the explosion will release gases. You'll have to talk to the Document Forgery Office to get your passport to get into the United States. Clearly this is going to require overtime, so you have to get prior approval for that."

Zawiki checked off his notes as he went. "The Finance Department has to approve the budget. They've moved, by the way, and won't be up and running until next month. The Financial Disbursement Office will have to agree about how to get the funds to you. Since the money will most likely go through a hawala system and eventually into a Swiss bank account, you'll need written approval from the Hawala Office, the European Department, and the office in charge of Switzerland, plus our newly formed Fund Dispensary Group. I almost forgot, since the financing is coming from the Crown Prince of Ombudai, you will need to talk to the Eastern Hemisphere Department and the desk in charge of Ombudai, and you'll need special permission from the front office, since the financing involves royalty. Of course, you can't start this process until you have travel orders, which you can get just as soon as I sign off on the proposal, but I can't do that right now since I have to go to a meeting."

Zawiki hefted himself up off the rug with the help of two aides. "Khaled, do you have that phone for Omar?" Zawiki asked one of the aides. Khaled handed Omar a cell phone. "That's for this operation, Omar. We'll get you the financial information after everyone has signed off." Zawiki waddled out of the conference cave.

Omar left the meeting feeling dazed. As he walked slowly back out to the main cave area, he longed for the whimsical early days of the Brotherhood, when sabotaging peanut farms using low-budget methods like weed planting and human fertilizer dumping could be carried out with hardly an hour's planning, the right diet, and a simple pre-wipe handshake between participants. Now he had to wind his way through Caliphate Crossing to sell his attack plan to eighteen different offices. He was briefly pulled out of his lamentation when he felt a bump against his shoulder. He turned to see an engorged woman holding a stack of papers and riding on a donkey that was weaving its way through the cave complex. He fell back into his despondency.

CHAPTER TWENTY
AJAKAR, PIGALLO

With Abdul and his goat safely out of the region, General Banja pleased with his new Mercedes, and the Gabimbian military better trained to handle a terrorism crisis, Victor returned to Ajakar Station.

He sat at his desk, annoyed that Joseph the Support Officer had once again switched out his chair. He had also placed a yellow police strip across the GS-15 chair, which sat empty against the wall. Victor switched them back, carefully unraveling the police strip so it wouldn't rip, and sat down just as Zed entered the shark tank. He sat in Victor's discarded chair, ripping the police tape. Victor winced.

"Director gave kudos for the exfil of Abdul."

"Really?" Victor said. Even he thought he sounded a little too excited.

"Don't bask in the glory. The kudos was for Director's team, not you. Called them 'the quarterbacks' of the operation. Thought it was a stellar example of how joint ops should be run." Zed wriggled and looked at the back of the chair. "What the fuck's wrong with this thing?" He looked back at Victor. "They are going to use it as a case study for the IÜD's Lessons Learned database. I guess true quarterbacks sit at desks in Washington. But what we did right here was to keep those quarterbacks so busy passing electronic paper back and forth that they couldn't interfere with what we were doing. You did the right thing getting him out quietly. The goat, too."

"I gave him my word."

"The goat?"

"Abdul."

"Good to see that still matters to some people. Next on the list," Zed changed the subject. "Director wants everyone to focus on a new terrorist organization. It seems this group has a global presence."

"How did I miss that? Did they appear overnight?"

"The FNU LNUs. They're everywhere and are likely hell bent on destroying America and the values we hold dear."

Victor smacked the palm of his hand against his forehead. "John Boy actually managed to get the seventh floor in a tizzy about the First Name Unknown Last Name Unkowns?"

"They are a grave threat to all we stand for and are now priority number one," Zed said in an exaggerated serious tone. "Among the many intelligence gaps Director wants filled: Why are there so many Mohammed LNUs? How do they keep each other straight in communications? Who is FNU Chang and how does he maintain a simultaneous presence in nearly every city in China? These are pressing questions, Victor. I expect you to drop everything and get on it immediately. Director is counting on you, as support, of course. The real work will be done back in Washington." He walked out.

Victor took a moment to recover from the conversation then looked down at the thumb drive Abdul had given him. He picked it up off his desk and twisted it in his fingers. He plugged it into his computer and began sifting through the files.

He saw several references to the Crown Prince of Ombudai and remembered with a pang how Director had ordered him to drop Axl Steiger as a potential source. One document in particular caught Victor's eye. It was a recent email to Omar al-Suqqit, referencing an attack in the United States and prevailing on al-Suqqit to travel to Rubblestan to finalize his plans with Core Central. Victor went immediately to Zed's office.

"Chief?"

"Hang on." Zed's fingers raced across the keyboard and he read out loud as he wrote a cable. "And thus Ajakar Station requests permission to purchase a new fleet of vehicles for Station personnel, so that they can more effectively tackle the threat posed by the troglodyte FNU LNUs present in West Africa."

"We're getting new cars?"

"I've been trying for a year to get us new cars. Mine has been repaired in Pigallo so many times now I think it's held together with chewing gum and rubber bands. The guy asked me for Scotch tape last time I was in there. If I tell Director we need to replace those hunks of junk out there because they no longer function, Director says no. If I say it's necessary to replace them to capture FNU LNUs, we're golden."

"You know no one at Director will know what a troglodyte is."

"It will keep them busy, having to look it up. What's up?"

"I've been going through those thumb drive docs from Abdul. Suqqit's going to Rubblestan."

"You got contacts out there?"

"A good friend handles a number of sources who can probably get info on Suqqit's visit."

"Then it looks like you're going to Rubblestan."

Victor went back to the shark tank and again switched chairs, rolling the GS-15 ergonomic beauty against the wall and replacing the yellow police ribbon as best he could across its seat. He dragged the GS-13 chair creaking back to his desk. Once he was seated on the rusty stool that passed as a chair for his grade level, he called in Joseph the Support Officer to start the paperwork to allow him to travel to Rubblestan.

CHAPTER TWENTY-ONE
CALIPHATE CROSSING, RUBBLESTAN

Omar sat on a cushion at Teahadi. Many Core Central warriors were taking their morning breaks, catching up with each other on the latest news and discussing developments of various operations. As he bit into a fig, Omar saw Akim approaching him.

"Brother!" Omar called out. "Emir of the Rubblestan Central Brigade. How good to see you. Please join me."

Akim sat down with a relieved huff and leaned over to give Omar a brotherly hug. "You look worn out, Emir Omar. I hope you are not ill."

"Not at all," Omar replied with a quiet voice. "But my sandals are worn and my feet are tired. I've no idea how many kilometers I've walked these past days trying to acquire the proper signatures for my plan."

"My brother, that is great news! Your operation is advancing then?"

"It seems that way. We've settled on a peanut refinery plant in Atlanta, Georgia. We've got someone on the inside and, of course,

Atlanta has a rather large Zuzuan population. We're not likely to stand out. I found an apartment to rent online. It has wonderful amenities. Cable TV, a community pool, and a dishwasher." Omar had not had a dishwasher since he had cut himself off from his wealthy family back in Zuzu. That dishwasher had been a tall beauty with doe eyes named Zeyna, and Omar had been smitten with her, although that had been against the rules. He wondered what his dishwasher in Atlanta would look like and if she would be as beautiful.

"Emir Omar, God be willing, your plan is well underway," Akim said.

"God may be willing, but the Housing Services Office is not. They have determined the apartment exceeds the limit set in the regulations by one square meter. I've appealed, of course, and argued they should make an exception. The apartment is excellent for its location, access, and commuting times to hardware stores and other suppliers. My appeal is on the agenda for the next housing meeting, which is scheduled to take place in two weeks. Then the leader of the office must sign off on the minutes of the meeting, but he is scheduled to be traveling at that time."

"And so it is here at Caliphate Crossing, brother. Just remember, patience is a virtue."

Omar didn't really believe that, but he clinked his teacup against Akim's as the two emirs toasted to the future success of Omar's operation.

CHAPTER TWENTY-TWO
FREEDOM RANCH, RUBBLESTAN

Victor gave Habibi a manly hug as he stepped off the transport plane.

"Long flight?" Habibi asked, taking in Victor's disheveled hair and sweaty face.

"A fourteen-hour commercial flight before this transport flight, and Director wouldn't let me fly business class."

"Budget cuts, my friend. It's expensive spreading democracy." Habibi led Victor toward the main compound. A sign at the entrance announced, "Welcome to Freedom Ranch!"

"So this is how we export freedom," Victor said. He looked at the twelve-foot-high walls adorned with curled razor wire.

"We're very good at it. At least that's what people on TV tell me." They passed the main building, which had once served as the Core leader's private home, and arrived at a metal shipping container. "Welcome to my palace."

They entered Habibi's windowless box and he threw Victor's khaki duffel bag onto a mattress on the floor. "That's your bed," he said. "This one's mine. If you snore or try to cuddle, I kick you out. Come on, I'll show you the rest of the place."

They went back outside. "We've got two separate living areas," Habibi said, pointing to the two sides of the compound. "That side is for the people who came to work. That side over there is for the people who came to get laid." Pineapple string lights were strewn across several of those metal boxes. A neon Bud Light sign flashed from a rooftop.

They moved deeper into the compound. Outside a Popeye's Chicken they passed a bulletin board advertising a pillow fight in Sector B that night, to be followed by a bonfire keg party. On their left, bright green leaves and intertwined branches accented with pink and yellow flowers formed an Eden-like tunnel.

"This way to the office," Habibi said, leading Victor into the lush opening.

Victor stepped out of the tunnel to the sounds of whooping laughter. An enormous swimming pool, filled with bright blue water, shimmered in the sun. A group of men, their muscles taut, held thong bikini-clad women on their shoulders in the pool. The women wrestled each other, giggling, and poured beer all around. Another young woman ran toward the pool, ripped off her T-shirt, and shrieked, "Freedom!" as she jumped topless into the water.

Victor and Habibi entered the main building and went up to the office. They opened the fire- and bulletproof door and walked in. They stopped short when they saw a small person in a traditional Rubblestani *pakoul* cap, loose trousers, and a tunic buried head first in a filing cabinet filled with classified documents. One of his feet was off the floor, he was dug in so far. Victor and Habibi both tensed, looked at each other, and silently drew their weapons.

"*Shakriya prustinya?*" Habibi said in his native Pashtu slang for, "What the fuck are you doing?"

The little feet kicked and fumbled as the man tried to pry loose.

"Slowly. Put down the documents," Habibi said.

The little man freed himself from the jaws of the cabinet and turned to face Habibi. He jumped when he saw the gun and papers flew out of his hands and rained down to the floor. "Habibi!" he screamed. "It's me!"

Habibi exhaled and lowered his gun. "Arnold, what the fuck are you doing wearing that shit and digging through our files? I almost shot you."

"What are you thinking, man?" Arnold was trembling. "It's *Shalwar Kameez* Day!"

"What the fuck is *Shalwar Kameez* Day?" Habibi asked.

"The ambassador told everyone to wear their *shalwar kameez* today. This, this clothing. To show the local workers how much we appreciate them." He was grabbing at his tunic.

"Christ," Habibi said. "Victor, Arnold," he said, introducing the two. "Arnold, Victor." Victor put his gun in his left hand and shook Arnold's hand with his right. He noticed Arnold's badge hanging on the outside of his *shalwar kameez*. The lanyard read, "What would Jesus do?"

"Listen, Arnold. We're gonna need a car tonight."

"No can do, Habibi."

"What do you mean no? We have a meeting tonight. We need a car."

"He's not cleared to go out in a car," Arnold said, pointing to Victor. "You didn't fill out form H1D5."

"Where's the fucking form? I'll fill it out now."

"You won't have time. It has to go back to Director."

"He'll just be a passenger. I'll drive."

"He still has to take the defensive vehicle passenger course."

"I won't bring him. I'll go by myself."

"Nice try, Habibi. You're very clever," he said, laughing and shaking a finger at Habibi. "But I already know you're going to bring him with you."

"Arnold, we need a car tonight. I don't have time for parallel parking courses or whatever the fuck it is."

"I'm sorry, Habibi. Director's rules. Just tell whoever you're meeting to come to the Freedom Zone. They're replaying yesterday's Redskins game over at the bar. He might like that."

"If he's seen coming into the Freedom Zone, he'll be killed," Habibi said.

"Then you can watch football without interruptions. Besides, he'll still be on our asset list. When Director does an accounting of how many sources we have, this guy will still count for this year. Which is great, because I'm up for promotion."

"But he'll be dead."

"It's a war, Habibi. People are going to die and we can't do anything about it."

***

That night, while most of Freedom Ranch was at the bonfire and keg party, Victor and Habibi snuck into the office. Arnold, who was always sure to let people know he worked late most nights, was asleep in front of his computer. Behind him, in a corner, several sets of car keys hung from hooks. Arnold snored as Habibi leaned over the desk and reached for a set of keys. He leaned too far and nearly knocked over a statue of Jesus that had a colorful lei around its neck. He pulled back, as Arnold shifted. Habibi tried to slide behind Arnold and the desk, where he managed to grab a set of car keys. He and Victor tiptoed out of the office, closing the door behind them with a soft click.

"We have to steal our own car?" Victor asked once they were outside.

"Do you think that's weird?" Habibi asked. "I think that's weird."

They got into a gray Toyota Forerunner. A bobble-head Jesus danced on the dashboard.

"That's Arnold's touch," Habibi said, flicking Jesus' head, which bobbled frantically. "He doesn't quite understand the subtleties of this war."

"Islamic extremism is a subtlety?"

"He also brought a crate full of Bibles to hand out to the locals at the embassy."

"How's that working out for him?"

"He doesn't have a lot of friends."

Habibi revved the engine and the two disappeared out the compound gate and into the night beyond.

***

Habibi and Victor drove through a small village and stopped in a deserted field, which was their rendezvous point with Source Akim. One of them had to stand outside the car as a signal to Akim that it was safe. They both checked their watches; they would wait four minutes, no more, and would have to abort if Akim didn't appear. Victor did a quick scan of the area, saw no one, and opened his door to get out. As he stepped out, an enormous black dog came racing out of nowhere, running toward Victor. The wild dog was baring its teeth, saliva flying out the sides of its mouth as it ran, and barking wildly.

Victor's eyes widened in fear as he screamed, "Holy shit!" He jumped back in the car and slammed the door. "Where the fuck did that come from?"

Habibi laughed. "What a beast!" The dog was jumping up on Victor's side of the car, trying to bite and claw through the window. "You should have seen your face!" he said, still laughing. "Wow! He's a big dog!"

Victor was breathing heavily. The dog backed away from the window and began circling the car, still growling.

"You can get out now," Habibi said. "Three minutes and counting. We gotta signal Akim."

"You get out," Victor said.

"Hell no. There's a giant rabid dog out there."

"I'm not going."

"You have to go. I just stole a car for you."

"That thing's gonna eat me alive. I can't be eaten by a dog. I go to Rubblestan and get killed by a dog? A terrorist, sure, I can handle that. An improvised explosive device? Shit happens in a war. But a fucking dog?"

"You want info on Suqqit or not? Get the fuck out of the car."

Victor looked around the inside of the car. "You got a stick or something?"

Habibi grabbed the bobble-head Jesus off the dashboard and slapped it into Victor's hand.

"Are you fucking crazy?" Victor said.

"It's the scariest thing in the car, trust me."

Victor took Jesus, whose head bounced with each movement, and held it as far in front of him as he could as he stepped out of the car. He swung Jesus this way and that as he scanned the area for the monster dog. He didn't hear a sound.

Suddenly, behind Victor, someone was screaming, "Open the door!" A Rubblestani man came running out from behind a shack, pursued by the giant black beast, which was biting at his heels. Akim dove into the back seat of the car just as Habibi opened it for him. Victor jumped back into the front.

The three men took a moment to catch their breath while the menacing dog circled the car outside. Finally, Victor stuck the bobble-head Jesus back on the dashboard.

"Akim, meet my partner, Victor." Habibi said. Victor and Akim shook hands. Habibi started driving. Akim pulled out a set of prayer beads. Jesus bobbled his head.

"Were you able to get the info on Omar al-Suqqit?" Habibi asked Akim as he maneuvered the car through the field and away from the dog.

"Yes," Akim said, fingering his prayer beads and looking at Jesus on the dashboard. "Now I know why you were asking about him. He's on his way to your United States." Victor and Habibi glanced at each other. "He's planning an operation at a peanut refinery plant. In Georgia. I always liked the sound of that state. Like a nice lady's name." The word rolled off Akim's tongue a few times before Habibi's look told him to continue with his information. "Something with explosives. He's got someone on the inside to help him."

"How do you know this?" Victor asked.

"I just had tea with him. We met a few weeks back at Emir Training. He's at Caliphate Crossing now, getting approvals for his operation. Why does his head move like that?" Akim pointed to the bobble-head Jesus.

"What approvals?"

"Dr. Zawiki has him running all over headquarters. They are being very careful since that cell in Buffalo was rounded up. Does the head ever stop moving?"

Victor put his hand on Jesus' head to steady it, to no avail. "What did you cover in the course?" he asked Akim.

"Typical leadership stuff. How to talk to your subordinates and motivate them. That kind of thing. I've got one guy, he can't grow a beard. He's tried, really hard. It's just not in his genes. But he's a hell of an explosives expert. Should he not be promoted just because he has no facial hair?"

"I hadn't really thought about that before."

"And two of my adherents, I can't get them to cooperate for anything. The first one caught the other one looking at the first one's wife. I understand the temptation. Her niqab was so bright she was just asking to be looked at. But it's your brother's wife! If I had known this was the type of thing I would have to deal with as emir..." Akim trailed off and rolled his eyes.

"Did al-Suqqit let on when the attack will take place?" Victor asked.

"He didn't share too much."

"You mentioned Zawiki," Habibi said.

"That guy," Akim said, shaking a finger in the air. "I have never seen someone get promoted so quickly. A few weeks ago he was in the DRZ, licking goat balls. Core Central Leadership loves him. That's how it is, you know. Take a corporate position at headquarters if you want to move up. Stay in the field, you're an unknown entity."

"He's at your headquarters? Doing what?" Victor asked.

"He's in charge of all ops for the African franchises. He's in charge of getting funding for al-Suqqit's project."

"Where's the money coming from?"

"No word on that yet, but I'll keep listening."

Habibi drove back around to the drop-off point, while Akim elaborated on the information he had gathered. Once at the drop-off point, Habibi reached under the seat and pulled out a bag. "Thanks for the info." He handed the bag to Akim. "For you."

Akim opened the bag and peered inside. "Black Label?"

"That's what you asked for," Habibi said.

"Can I try Johnnie Walker Blue next time?"

"I'll see what I can do."

"And is this the November issue? You can't beat Miss November. November is always the best one. Thank you, my friend." He threw his prayer beads into the bag with the whiskey and Playboy magazine.

Akim jumped out of the car and ran to the shack, just as the dog came around a corner barking.

***

Victor and Habibi returned to Freedom Ranch to write up the information from Source Akim.

"We should leave out the part about stealing a car," Habibi said. "And maybe the stuff about chasing off a rabid dog with a bobble-head Jesus."

"I think that part kind of makes me look like a hero," said Victor.

"We need to request permission to capture both Suqqit and Zawiki."

"Highlight in there that Akim is a stellar source. He's been vetted and provided corroborated info and all that. Don't give Director a way out." The two case officers huddled together at a computer, whispering. "And remember the tearline for the FBI. Suqqit and Zawiki should be placed on the Most Wanted Terrorists list."

Arnold remained asleep at his desk, a puddle of drool under his cheek.

***

The following day, Victor and Habibi set out early to meet with another of Habibi's sources, Qissam. The meeting site was in a rocky valley several hours' drive from Freedom Ranch and a full day's walk from Qissam's village.

"You look tired," Victor said to Habibi. "I thought you were coming to the war zone for a rest. No commute and all that."

"No traffic on this commute at least. Except that guy there on the donkey." Habibi nodded toward the side of the road. "I could be completely stuck on the Beltway right now. Maybe I'll bring back a donkey. A donkey on the Beltway. I bet it would be faster." They bumped along, passing the man on the donkey.

"What's up with the sunglasses?" Victor asked.

"What's wrong with my sunglasses?" Habibi asked, readjusting them and looking annoyed.

"They're pink."

"They're Gucci. I got them just before I came to Rubblestan."

"You wore pink Gucci sunglasses to a war?"

"Fuck you."

"No. I like it. Manly. I'm sure the locals won't try to fuck with you at all."

Habibi stretched his back. "Fuck you again. And fuck my back."

"What's wrong with your back? Is it rebelling against your pink sunglasses?"

"I took medication this morning. It's killing me."

"The medication?"

"My back."

"Is this your way of asking me for a massage?"

"No, asshole. I just wonder if I should be driving."

"Because of your back?"

"Because of the medication."

"What's wrong with the medication?"

"The warning says it can make you sleepy and you shouldn't handle large machinery."

"And you thought it was a good idea to take the medication this morning, just before driving halfway across a hostile country to meet a source in a dangerous outpost?"

"My back hurt."

"And your gun?"

"No, my gun doesn't hurt."

"No, do you think you should be handling a firearm while falling asleep from back pain medication?"

"It's maybe not the best idea I've ever had. But really, what am I going to hit? With the car or the gun? Maybe a donkey. That's it. There's nothing else out here except rubble."

They drove on in silence, taking in the piles of rubble that gave the country its moniker. After a while, Habibi spoke.

"Are you hungry? I think this medication is making me hungry."

They split a pork sausage sandwich they had packed and passed a bottle of water back and forth. A few hours later, they arrived at the pick-up point.

"Get in the back," Habibi said to Victor.

"Why?"

"Qissam likes the front seat."

Victor hopped into the back seat. A frail looking man in blue robes floated up to the car and got in. Victor saw he had scaly skin and a number of his fingernails looked as though they were barely holding on to his fingers.

"My friend, I am so sorry about last time," Qissam said to Habibi. "I am afraid it could not be avoided."

"Don't worry, Qissam. As long as everything is all right?"

"I could not come. They called an emergency meeting at the base. If I had not been there, they would have noticed. I am sorry you had to drive so far and I could not make it."

"Don't worry about me, as long as you're safe. What happened at the meeting?"

Qissam looked back at Victor while chewing on one of his hanging fingernails. He turned to Habibi and gave a head nod toward Victor. "Who's this?"

"My partner. What happened at the meeting?"

Qissam picked at some of his peeling skin. "General Quereshi, he told his group to keep the heat off the Core."

"Quereshi? The head of counterterrorism for the Rubblestani Service for Intelligence?" Habibi asked.

"That's the one. Quereshi invited Core Central Leadership to his country house just outside the capital. Right next to our military academy. Said they could stay there as long as they wanted.

He ordered his RSI troops to help the Core. You might want to secure your supply routes. I think they want to blow them up."

"Quereshi was just in Washington asking for more money."

"He loves those trips, and the money and gifts that come with them. He's hoping you guys never leave Rubblestan because he loves all the donations that go with it. I heard his collection of rare wines has increased tenfold with the 'contributions' he siphons off from the aid packages. But, you know, he was helping the Core years ago, before you guys decided the Core was evil. That was just good domestic politics for him. Still is. He'll still be here in Rubblestan once you guys leave. And so will the Core." He handed Habibi a compact disc. "As I said, watch your supply routes."

"The Rubblestan government signed an accord with us to allow us to use those routes."

"You Americans only have to live with the Core for a few years. We Rubblestanis are stuck with them forever." Qissam got out of the car and walked away. One of his fingernails had fallen on the front seat.

Habibi started driving again.

"You can come back up front," he said to Victor.

Victor looked at the fingernail and flakes of skin. "No, I'm good back here."

Habibi glanced back at Victor and at the seat. "Oh, please. It's nothing. He's got leprosy, so what? He gives me good info."

"He's got leprosy?"

"What do you have against lepers?"

"The fact that they have leprosy."

He brushed the remnants of Qissam off the seat. "Come on."

Victor crawled into the front seat, visibly uncomfortable.

"It's a myth, Victor. You can't catch leprosy just by touching where a leper sat. Chill out."

They drove back toward Freedom Ranch with Victor curled almost into a ball in the front seat, afraid to touch anything.

***

Victor and Habibi stood outside the office door punching different numbers on the coded keypad.

"There are too many," Habibi complained, bent over the numbered pad. "Every door has a code. How is a normal human being supposed to remember them all? Even the bathroom has a code lock on it now. I almost shit my pants last week trying to remember how to open the fucking door." He kept punching in different numbers.

The door swung open and Arnold came out. Habibi immediately removed his finger from the keypad and stood up straight. He and Victor walked in as though they had just arrived.

Habibi logged on to his computer and moaned when he saw how many cables had come in since they were last in the office. He scrolled through, reading off the highlights for Victor.

"The Office of Security is forcibly relocating the geese in Director's courtyard. Someone finally realized they were Canadian, I guess." He continued scanning the cable headlines. "John Boy got an Exceptional Performance Award for his FNU LNU link chart analysis. Kudos, John Boy. Oh, God." Habibi froze.

"What is it?" Victor asked.

"Director wants to share the information about Suqqit and Zawiki's whereabouts with the Rubblestani Service for Intelligence."

"The RSI? You're shitting me," Victor said. He leaned over Habibi's shoulder to see the screen.

"Director's refusing a capture operation. Wants to vet Akim and get more info by passing what we have to the RSI."

Without a word, Victor and Habibi stood up and walked to the chief's office. Wally had been in the business for years. He boasted about having reached the senior service before turning forty-five, but the gossip was that he had achieved that only after he had threatened to sue the organization for discriminating against him for being one-fifteenth Armenian. His evidence was that there were, in fact, very few Armenians in the senior ranks.

Victor and Habibi walked into his office. Wally was on the secure phone back to Washington but motioned for them to sit down.

"No, listen, Joan. I told you. Paris. I won't settle for anything less than Paris," Wally said. "I don't care if he has been doing this longer. You promised me Paris. That's the only reason I agreed to this Rubblestan thing." He paused, listening to Joan on the other end of the phone. "I understand he won the Presidential Medal of Freedom. No one disputes he won that. I was at the ceremony when he got the plastic watch. But that doesn't mean he deserves Paris. I could have brought down a whole sleeper cell in Germany, too. But nobody asked me to. Besides, I'm stuck here. How am I supposed to stop a sleeper cell of terrorists if I'm here in Rubblestan? Now he looks like a hero. Listen, Joan. Paris. That's it. End of conversation." He hung up and sat down behind his desk. "Where the hell have you guys been?"

"Meeting sources."

"Where?"

"Outside the Freedom Zone."

Wally stared at them a moment. "I didn't realize we were doing that. Huh. Weird. Anyway, what's up?"

"We just saw the cable from Director about sharing the info on Suqqit and Zawiki with RSI. You know we can't pass that to them."

"Of course we can pass it to them. Of course I already passed it to them. Why do the work ourselves, when they can do it for us? You know how it is. If we actually do ops, something might go wrong. And there goes Paris for me." He leaned back in his plush leather chair and put his feet up on the desk.

"You already passed it? Chief, RSI is playing both sides. We can't trust anything they tell us. They'll tip off Suqqit and Zawiki."

"Guys, we pay the RSI's salaries. I met personally with General Quereshi on this one. He assured me he would do everything he could to capture these two."

"Quereshi isn't reliable!" Victor almost yelled, clenching his hands into fists and shooting up to his feet, unable to control his anger. "This is the guy who has a longer and longer shopping list every time he meets with us. The same guy who fed weapons and money to the Core before the attacks and probably still does. These guys have been in bed together for more than a decade. And you trust he's going to tell you the truth about Suqqit and Zawiki?"

"Now there's a cynical view, Victor. Thanks for that revisionist history. Our relationship with RSI is solid as a rock, and I have a very close and personal relationship with General Quereshi and quite frankly, I'm offended to hear you talk like that. I shared the information with him and I'm quite satisfied with the response I got back and I will be informing Director of that in a cable."

Victor sat back down and rubbed his temples. "We just met with Source Qissam. Just yesterday. Qissam. Who has been a source for years. Who is fully vetted. Whose information has been right time and time again. The RSI is working against us. Quereshi is working against us. He gave us proof. And he's just one source. There are others who corroborate the info."

Habibi looked at Wally. "What was Quereshi's response?"

"That the RSI looked for Suqqit and Zawiki but couldn't find them," Wally said.

"Oh my god," Victor said in disbelief.

"They said they couldn't find the location," Wally added.

"That message you passed included geo-coordinates," Habibi said. "How could they not find the location? Or is the only piece of equipment we haven't given them a GPS? Christ, my watch has a GPS. Should I give it to Quereshi?"

"The one piece of equipment they refuse to use, except probably to track us. Shit, soon they'll be shooting at us with bullets we supplied them," Victor said.

"I don't understand where this is coming from," Wally said. "For me, it's a very satisfactory answer. They looked. They didn't find them. Now we're all off the hook and don't have to do anything."

Victor and Habibi walked out of Wally's office. They knew it: Suqqit was gone.

CHAPTER TWENTY-THREE
CALIPHATE CROSSING, RUBBLESTAN

Omar ordered a mint tea to go and headed down the hall toward Zawiki's office. Zawiki had put up several new motivational posters. The first poster depicted a young man about to pull the pin out of his explosives belt. In large, sharp letters under the picture was the word COMMITMENT. The next poster showed a woman carrying a baby with a bomb in its diaper onto a bus. Under the picture, it said, DEDICATION.

Omar peeked into Zawiki's office. The fleshy Core lieutenant was lying naked and face down on a massage table, a towel draped across his puffy buttocks. He was up to his elbow in a bag of popcorn, which he shoved in his mouth while a man in a Rubblestani Army uniform rubbed Zawiki's oiled up back.

"Come in, Omar," Zawiki said when he saw Omar at the door. "Have a seat. This is General Quereshi, from the Rubblestani Service for Intelligence."

Omar nodded toward the general, who nodded back as he poured more poppy-scented oil onto Zawiki.

119

"General Quereshi here was just telling me about some information he has come across. It seems the Americans are watching us and have asked our good friend the general here to bring us in."

"No need to change your plans, gentlemen," Quereshi said. He took Zawiki's right foot into his hands and began kneading it gently. "I just thought I should inform you. Professional courtesy and all that. We've furnished them with an appropriate response. You men can continue on your path with no worries."

Omar looked at Zawiki. "The operation shall continue?"

"It shall advance and be glorious! Why do you worry?"

"We're on their radar now," Omar said.

"Yes, but they sold that radar to the general here."

"Actually, doctor, they just gave it to us," Quereshi said. "They're giving away all kinds of technology these days. Billion-dollar aid packages just overflowing with technology and striped lollipops."

Zawiki and Quereshi laughed together, as the general began rubbing the doctor's other foot.

"Thank you, gentlemen," Omar said. "I'll move on to the next phase then."

"Before you go, Omar," Zawiki said. "I trust you understand that, should your operation succeed, Core Central will run all associated media and public relations campaigns."

"Why can't the Core in the Desert do that? It's our operation."

"The Core wants to be heard as one voice. For any international strike, all franchises are required to relinquish their propaganda activities to Core Central. If you carry out an internal strike, in your region, we leave the outreach to you. But you understand, international attacks will be run out of Rubblestan."

"The same applies if we fail in our endeavor?"

Zawiki laughed. "If you fail, the Core in the Desert shall take full responsibility for the planning and attempted execution of the operation. Core Central will disavow your efforts and refer to you as Lone Wolves."

"I understand," Omar said. His frustration was mounting and he took a deep breath to calm himself. He exited Zawiki's office. The sound of Zawiki's relaxed moans faded into the distance.

CHAPTER TWENTY-FOUR
FREEDOM RANCH, RUBBLESTAN

Victor was exhausted and drained, between the adrenaline highs of his source meetings and the depressing lows of feeling those efforts had been undercut by a Washington policy that was much bigger than him. He was leaving in one hour for the long trip back to Director—a new requirement; all employees had to fly to their home stations from Director, ostensibly in an effort to compartmentalize which overseas stations were working together, although this had resulted in officers flying from their home station in, for example, London to Paris for a meeting, then having to fly to Washington before returning to London, because apparently only spies flew round trip from London to Paris and an unnecessary jaunt to Washington looked less suspicious. Victor went into the station to say goodbye to Habibi.

"The White House just announced a multi-billion-dollar financial aid package for Rubblestan," Habibi said. "Third one this year."

"Our most reliable partner in the Total War on Terror," Victor said.

"We're going to be delivering sacks of cash to the Rubblestani government. That's not a metaphor, by the way. Actual sacks of cash. Arnold is in the other room filling them up."

"To build schools and infrastructure, I'm sure."

"We're also giving them weapons."

"Which they'll never use against us."

"The White House is making sure of that. Asked Rubblestan to name someone to monitor the disbursements, to make sure they go to the right places. Of course, the president of Rubblestan named his brother."

"Naturally."

"The head of RSI will be visiting Director next week. He'll get a personal tour of the ops center, the nerve center for the war."

"He needs to see that, to know where we are so he can aim his new weapons accordingly."

Habibi gave Victor a quick hug. "Good seeing you, man. Safe trip."

CHAPTER TWENTY-FIVE
WASHINGTON, DC

Victor swiped his ID card and entered Director's headquarters. It had been a long trip. He had chosen a somewhat circuitous route to Washington from Rubblestan, but it beat the risk of taking the same flight as all of his colleagues, whose trips in and out were now so regular that the RSI had started monitoring the passenger manifests, noting down the names of all the American Embassy employees and the likely CYA officers and tucking away that information for when it might come in handy. Even waiting at the airport before departing, Victor did his best to distance himself from them, in an effort to keep his identity secret from the RSI. His colleagues were easy to spot in their camouflage cargo pants, Under Armour T-shirts, and dark Ray-Ban sunglasses.

He picked up a coffee at Starbucks and headed to the Travel Office to make his arrangements to fly back to Pigallo, where he hoped to catch a trace of al-Suqqit once again. The Travel Office had other plans.

"I'm afraid I can't issue you any travel orders, Mr. Caro." The woman behind the desk tapped at her keyboard. She used the knuckles of her two index fingers to type, as her fingernails curled out more than an inch. They were each decorated with an American flag and glitter. The two middle fingers had words on them. One said, NEVER, the other said, FORGET. She looked up at Victor and said, "According to the computer, you're dead."

"I'm not dead. I'm standing right here."

"That's what you're telling me, but the computer is telling me something very different. I can't process any travel orders for you if you're dead."

"It's a valid point, Kinesha," Victor said, looking at the nameplate perched on her cubicle. She had decorated it with pictures of her cats. "But you see, I'm not dead. I'm right here. Alive and well."

"I'm sorry. As far as we're concerned, you're dead. If the computer tells us something, we can't do anything about it. I'm so sorry for you and your family. How did it happen? So young, so sad."

"Tell me, Kinesha. Is there a way to convince the computer I'm not dead?"

"Maybe try your HR officer," Kinesha suggested as she tried to pry open a Tupperware box of leftovers without breaking a nail.

"Thank you so much for your help."

Victor went next door to the Human Resources Department. It was empty except for one woman, who was on her way out. Victor stopped her. "Excuse me, can you help me?"

"You gotta make it quick," she said. "It's Amish Appreciation Day. I'm on my way to the quilt show in Corridor F."

"I need to prove I'm not dead so I can get travel orders issued, so I can go back to my station."

She ruffled through a stack of papers in a plastic file holder hanging on the wall and handed a form to Victor. "Take this to the medical office. The doctor there has to prove you're not dead. Then bring it back here for a stamp. Then you can get your travel orders."

Victor looked at form 14-F-MED, titled, "Proclamation of Lack of Decease."

"Thanks," he said.

"Now you know where the form is for next time," the woman said, rushing out to go to the quilt show.

Victor walked to the medical office and showed the receptionist his form. "I need to see the doctor to prove I'm not dead."

"Not a problem. Just a moment," she said.

The doctor ushered Victor into an exam room and quickly perused his file.

"Let's have a look. Undress, please, and put on this robe."

Victor did so, and the doctor proceeded to give him a full physical examination. The doctor finished feeling the glands in Victor's neck then set about writing in Victor's file. He was writing a lot.

"Everything OK, doc? Do I pass the living test?"

"I'm going to clear you, but with the caveat that you need a follow-up exam with your personal physician."

"You're a doctor, and you see I'm alive."

"I'm only here as an insurance policy to Director. I need the backup of your physician to tell us you won't die."

"My doctor can't guarantee that. He can only guarantee that I'm not dead now, nor have I ever been."

"If he is unwilling to fill out this form, then you'll be stuck here. I'm also going to direct you to see the psychiatrist, because we need to make sure you're in the proper mental state to travel back to your post and start up again with the stresses of your work. It must have been quite a shock to find out you were dead." He handed Victor a stack of forms and sent him on his way.

CHAPTER TWENTY-SIX
SOMEWHERE IN THE AIR BETWEEN RUBBLESTAN AND THE DEMOCRATIC REPUBLIC OF ZUZU

The whir of the Gulfstream, which the government of Rubblestan had chartered for him, had lulled Omar into a relaxed state. He reclined his leather seat and settled in for the long flight back to the Democratic Republic of Zuzu. The flight attendant offered him a warm cup of camel milk and he watched as she reached up for a glass, her long robe crawling up just enough to allow Omar a glimpse of her bare ankle.

He reflected yet again on his operation. As Omar was leaving Caliphate Crossing, he learned that the finance office had finally approved the attack. Zawiki had secured the funds from the Crown Prince after a quick trip to Marbella, Spain, where Zawiki had participated in numerous activities not technically allowed by his faith but forgiven in instances meant to forward the Almighty's agenda.

But Omar was worried. The Crown Prince had to be under intense scrutiny, given his role in the big attacks and his not so tacit support of the Core, including using his son as a courier between Ombudai and Rubblestan. Recently he had been pouring money into the DRZ, propping up bin Fuqin while buying real estate to launder his money before sending it to Switzerland. He was too high profile, Omar felt. On the other hand, his plan could now go forward. He sipped his camel milk and walked through the plan again.

CHAPTER TWENTY-SEVEN
WASHINGTON, DC

Victor walked around the parking lot clicking the alarm on the key to his rental car. All the cars looked the same out here, and it was difficult to tell one parking row from the other. He had Row EE stuck in his head, but was that where he had parked yesterday or today? Because he couldn't find the car there today. What kind of car was he looking for anyway? Was it the white Dodge? Or was that the car he had rented the last time he was here? It was all a giant blur. He had been back to Director, parked in this lot, and lost a rental car in the sea of rental cars in the lot so many times over the past ten years. Finally, he heard the squawk of an alarm and saw the lights of a gold Dodge Neon flicker two rows away.

He drove out of the compound and was a mile down the road when a policeman pulled him over. He could see the young cop approaching the car very slowly, with his hand on his holster.

"Salam, sir. Slowly, please, put your hands on the steering wheel where I can see them."

"Salam? What seems to be the problem, officer?"

"I'll ask the questions, sir. Which mosque are you heading to or coming from?"

"Excuse me?" Victor was stunned.

"We don't see your type around these parts much. Where are you going?"

"Are you pulling me over because I have a beard?" Victor glanced at himself in the rearview mirror. He had meant to shave since he had come back from Rubblestan but it hadn't been a priority with all the other things he needed to do, like prove he wasn't dead and find a trace of the terrorist he had managed to lose. It was very common for the guys in Rubblestan to grow out their beards. It certainly helped them blend in a bit in the market, but also, with so few women around, standards of personal hygiene dropped significantly.

"We all have one god, sir. This isn't about religion. This isn't about your beard. That would be profiling. I'm pulling you over because you look suspicious, driving around here in a rental car. Show me your license and registration. Slowly."

Victor pulled out his license and saw his clean-shaven face in the photo. The cop took the information back to his car and Victor could see him talking on his radio. Victor stroked his beard without realizing it. A few minutes later, the police officer returned.

"You're free to go, Mr. Caro. For now. But I am required to tell you that your information has been passed to the Department of Homeland Security."

"Why?"

"That's not information we are obligated to share. I suggest you think carefully about where you shop and the business you get involved in. You have a good day. Salam."

Victor went back to his hotel and shaved.

***

It was not until a few days later that Victor learned of the wider consequences of the well-meaning officer's actions. Having successfully gotten his personal physician to agree that Victor was not dead, he returned to Director to hand in his paperwork and try again to get his plane ticket to return to Pigallo. He went back to Kinesha in the travel office. She was sharpening a pencil in an electric sharpener, holding the pencil between her thumb and index finger; the other fingers flared out so they wouldn't get nicked.

Victor put on his biggest smile. "Hi, Kinesha! How are you? How are the cats?"

Kinesha perked up. "My cats are great, thank you very much! What can I help you with today?"

"I need to get a plane ticket to Pigallo."

"Let's get that ready for you." She punched in Victor's information. Her smile dropped. "Mr. Caro, I am pleased you are not dead, but I'm afraid you've been put on the Terrorist Watch List."

"No, Kinesha. I work here."

She gave Victor an apprehensive look and picked up the phone, still being careful with her fingernails. "I have to call security."

"Not necessary, Kinesha. I'll work this out with my boss."

Victor walked out and went to the Counterterrorism Department. In a back corner was a filing cabinet. He opened it, sifted through some of the contents, and pulled out a plastic bag. He dumped what was inside on a table. It was an alias package he always kept ready: eyeglasses, hair gel, a baseball cap, a wallet with a driver's license and credit cards, and a passport, all with the name of Stan Moakley from Pennsylvania. Admittedly, Victor never imagined he would need this alias package to fool his own government, but still, he always knew it would be a handy thing to have.

He donned the disguise and grabbed his new documents. As he exited the Counterterrorism Department offices, security guards were rushing in, looking for Victor Caro. He went back to see Kinesha. Five minutes later, he had in his hand a plane ticket for Stan Moakley to travel to Pigallo.

CHAPTER TWENTY-EIGHT
AJAKAR, PIGALLO

Victor landed at Ajakar International Airport in the early morning. The heat of Pigallo stung his nose. He ached all over. He had just spent the last ten hours squashed between a large man who had not showered in days and a round woman holding a chicken. Apparently, the Pigallo route was not the airline's top priority, and they had assigned their oldest plane and unhappiest flight attendants to it. The televisions didn't work. Neither did the lights. At one point, a flight attendant took a piece of chewing gum out of her mouth and stuck it on the door of the overhead compartment in an effort to keep it shut.

He was still contemplating the wretched flight when he realized he was the last one at the baggage carousel, the conveyor belt going round and round, empty. At last, through the ripped plastic strips that separated the outdoors from inside, he saw his luggage. And his underwear. And his socks. Everything he had packed was falling out of the shredded bag, like entrails hanging out of a slaughtered animal. He scooped it up and walked to immigration.

Sitting at a small desk was Babaka, a young immigration officer that Victor knew well. They had worked together several times trying to piece together an effective border control policy for Pigallo. His olive green uniform was too large for his skinny frame and his thick glasses made his eyes look too big.

"Mr. Caro! I have just heard the terrible news!"

"Babaka, how are you? What terrible news?"

"We just received a new Terrorist Watch List from your embassy, and there I see your name. I say, yes, is true Mr. Caro taught me how to shoot out a tire. Is true he likes the ladies. But Mr. Caro is no terrorist."

"Thanks, Babaka. Now I am ready to get home and get cleaned up and get back to the office."

"I am sorry, Mr. Caro. I cannot let you pass. You are a terrorist. Your own government says so. You always tell me your government knows better than mine. I should listen to your government."

"No, Babaka. In this case, my government is wrong."

"Mr. Caro, how can you say United States is wrong? I love United States!"

"Babaka, here's my passport."

Babaka picked up Stan Moakley's passport. He looked at Victor with astonishment. "You are not Mr. Caro at all! I am so sorry, Mr. Moakley, for the confusion!" Babaka stamped the passport and wrote on three different pages with a grand sweep of his hand. "Mr. Moakley, welcome to my country!"

CHAPTER TWENTY-NINE
NUAKABATU, DEMOCRATIC REPUBLIC OF ZUZU

Omar sat down in the Shwarma Shack under a poster of bin Fuqin dressed in military fatigues and surrounded by red flowers. He took out his phone and pulled up the advertisement for the apartment in Atlanta. He punched in the credit card number he had received at Caliphate Crossing and immediately got an email confirming that the apartment would be rented to him beginning next month. He took a bite of falafel.

He turned when he heard the door of the Shwarma Shack open, and he saw a young woman covered head to toe in bright cascading robes. Her headscarf was a vibrant magenta and sat just far enough back to reveal a few dark strands of her hair. She was accompanied by a short man wearing a fez and carrying a clipboard.

"Leyla," Omar said gently as he stood to greet her. "Please, sit. You must be exhausted after such a long flight."

Leyla was the daughter of one of Omar's lieutenants. She had moved to the United States on a student visa with a scholarship to study agriculture and had landed a job at the targeted peanut refinery. She would drive the truck into the facility.

"Hello, Omar!" she said breathlessly, too excited to sit down. "This is Faruk..."

Before she could finish, Faruk threw both hands in the air and embraced Omar. "Yes! I am Faruk!" His voice was high-pitched and he dragged out the sound of his name, *Faruuuuuuuk.*

"I've chosen him to direct my martyr video," Leyla said, bouncing on her tiptoes.

"What an honor, Mr. Faruk. Your reputation precedes you," Omar said. "I've heard you called the Roman Polanski of the Middle East."

"That was never proved," Faruk said. "The young boy was just an assistant."

"In terms of filmmaking, I mean."

"I've always loved filmmaking. It's its own form of immortality, for those of us who choose not to join the Martyr Program."

"People contribute to the struggle in different ways," said Omar. "You can be proud."

Omar's phone rang and he excused himself, leaving Leyla and Faruk to discuss her martyr masterpiece. He glanced at the number. *Why is Zawiki calling me?*

"I've got a task for you," Zawiki said. Omar could hear him chewing on the other end of the line. "We've been following the Great Enemy's appropriations process for the Department of Homeland Security. Did you know Colorado got homeland security funds to buy new ski gear for its ski patrol? To look out for eco-terrorists. The Great Enemy is creative, I'll give it that."

"What does this have to do with me?" Omar asked, trying to get Zawiki back on track.

"The Kansas town of Argonia just got five million dollars for prophylaxis against infectious bovine rhinotracheitis. The virus could wipe out entire fields of cows," Zawiki said. "Core Central would like you to get some. At least ten vials. It's a West Africa specialty."

"You said the Great Enemy already has protection against the virus."

"Core Central Leadership is making it a top priority to show the Great Enemy that we've thought of everything they've thought of, even if they have already implemented counter-measures. If the Great Enemy decides to protect against it, we must prove we were already planning it. We don't want to look weak on terrorism."

"We're quite busy here organizing our next nuptials."

The Core had begun using the word "nuptials" as a code for "attack." Previously, they had used the word "marriage," but when an unmanned drone dropped Hellfire missiles on someone's actual wedding, the group changed the code word.

"I understand, but Core Central Leadership considers it a top priority. I don't want to be the one who has to stand in front of them and tell them we didn't have a technology the Great Enemy protected against. Will you get it?"

"I'll get it," Omar said. He clicked off his phone and turned back to Leyla and Faruk, who were discussing her most photogenic angles.

CHAPTER THIRTY
AJAKAR, PIGALLO

From outside the door to Ajakar Station, Victor could hear a loud banging sound, like a shoe on a table, keeping a constant rhythm. It was interrupted by a scream of frustration and a moment of silence. Then it began anew.

Victor punched in the code to the door and walked in to see Zed at his desk, pounding his forehead against his computer monitor. He stopped for a second, glanced at Victor, and went back to it.

"Good day, chief?"

"Just living the dream, my friend." He stopped again and turned to Victor. "You see all these flashing chat windows?" He pointed to his monitor. "That's for us. We're being sent on a mission. We're being ordered to render a guy out of Gabimbia."

"What?"

"The crotch burrowing squirrels in Legal won't let us meet with a highly connected banker who could track major terrorist funds because he eats sauerkraut. But in all their wisdom, they have deemed it appropriate to make a guy disappear from the streets."

"Who?"

"Sit down."

"Who, chief?" Victor remained standing.

"FNU LNU."

Victor rolled the information around in his head for a full five seconds before slumping into the chair opposite Zed. He began banging the back of his head against the wall.

"You feel my pain now," Zed said.

"Are they insane? FNU LNU doesn't exist."

"That's a detail that seems to have been lost on Director. This is blessed by the seventh floor."

"A trainee created that threat out of ignorance."

"Better to have ignorance propel us into action than to look ignorant for not having acted until it was too late. You don't want the evidence to be a mushroom cloud, do you?"

"That's bullshit."

"I know it's bullshit. You know it's bullshit. But it's an order from the very top. I mean the *very* top."

"The White House?"

"It's an election year. Gotta look tough."

"By kidnapping a nobody off the street?"

"By capturing terrorists and getting actionable intelligence so that freedom can ring again."

"I see. Yet when we wanted to catch Suqqit and Zawiki, who we know are terrorists, by the way—do we know if FNU LNU is a terrorist?"

"A peanut investor, but continue."

"When we wanted to catch two known terrorists, Director decided to hand that over to the RSI."

"That's called strengthening relations with our allies."

"But this peanut investor, we'll let him be our problem."

"So we can bask in the glory of having stopped the next attack."

"We don't know if he's even planning an attack."

"Director can't take the chance of waiting to find out."

"In the meantime, while I'm off rendering the world's most dangerous peanut investor with no name from Gabimbia, Suqqit continues with his plans."

"It will give you a project when we get back. Do you have personal liability insurance? The Agency probably won't cover our lawyers' fees when we get sued."

"Fuck me."

"There'll be time for that later, Victor. We leave tonight."

CHAPTER THIRTY-ONE
GABIMBIA

Once again, Victor was flying toward Gabimbia, only this time he and Zed were in a private Learjet with leather seats and gold accouterments. Zed had arranged to rent it using various front companies through a jet-share in Seattle. The complexity and price tag gave it more gravitas than the idea of snatching a FNU LNU out of a country most Americans had never heard of.

Victor was tense and Zed was quiet as they flew toward the sliver of land that was the country of Gabimbia.

"We have to do this quietly," Zed had said to Victor before they took off. "In and out. If this guy is indeed a terrorist, we don't want his asswipe associates to know he's been taken for a ride and is being politely asked a few questions. If he's not a terrorist, well, that would look pretty bad on the front page of *The Washington Post*. Not to mention those pansies over at State. They'd get their panties all tied in a knot if this were to turn into a diplomatic incident."

After only a few short minutes, they began their descent, circling down over the quiet, dark, and only airstrip in Gabimbia. Victor looked out his window and saw that single, sad plane sitting at the end of the runway, its squishy tires deflated, almost melting on the tarmac. "The mighty Gabimbian air force," Victor said.

The Learjet settled over the runway and began coming down fast when Victor heard the pilot say to no one in particular, "Brakes out." He said it like he was talking about the weather matter of factly, as if he were saying, "Raining out." Victor looked across the aisle at Zed, who looked slightly amused.

A thunderous clap broke the silence and the plane shook as the wheels slammed down on the runway. The pilot flipped switches and pulled up on the brakes. Through the plane's windshield, Victor could see the Gabimbian air force plane perched pathetically at the end of the airstrip. The Learjet was heading straight toward it.

"Holy shit," Victor said. The Learjet kept lurching forward. "We're going to destroy this country's entire air force."

Zed muffled a laugh.

The Learjet continued hurdling toward the little plane.

"France is going to be pissed off," Zed said.

"What about Gabimbia?"

"Yep. Them too." Zed paused. "You write that cable."

Victor was leaning back in his seat and pushing his foot into the floor in an effort to physically will the plane to stop.

Gabimbia's air force was just ahead, fifty feet, twenty feet. The pilot continued his struggle. Fifteen feet, ten feet, five feet. The Learjet rolled to a stop, its nose kissing the nose of the air force plane.

Victor exhaled.

Zed yelled up to the pilot, "A masterful display of your piloting prowess, Roger. Thanks for that."

He grabbed a black ski mask and pulled it over his head. Victor followed suit and they opened the plane's door. The air was so thick, Victor immediately choked.

"Zed, why the fuck are we wearing wool ski masks in the middle of the hottest fucking place on Earth?"

"Director's idea of continuity. Blanket regulation. All renditions have to use black wool ski masks after what happened in Kosovo."

"What happened in Kosovo?"

"They snatched a guy off the street wearing masks made from hemp. Trying to be environmental. When the interrogator lit up a cigarette, the mask caught fire. Word got back to Congress we were providing enemy combatants with marijuana. Funniest transcription of an interrogation I've ever seen, though. The guy was begging for Cheetos."

"Lowest common denominator, if you ask me."

"I didn't," Zed said, and he lumbered down the plane's stairs.

The jet's engines shut down and everything went quiet. For the first time, Victor thought that maybe they could pull this off without the entire country knowing they had been here. He scanned the area around the airstrip. No one. It was silent, until the pilot Roger, behind Victor on the stairs, said to no one in particular, "Reverse thrust is out. Can't back this baby up." He jumped down to the airstrip and observed the two planes. They were nose to nose; barely a baby's breath could pass between them. "Gonna have to back one up so I can turn around."

Victor began walking toward the hut next to the airstrip, leaving Zed and Roger at the plane. He heard nothing but his own footsteps and then, a moment later, Zed and Roger's grunting as they attempted to push the Gabimbian air force plane back a few feet.

Victor looked at them, muttered a "fuck" under his breath, and continued toward the hut, where his good friend General Banja was waiting with FNU LNU. Victor sensed he was being watched and turned around again. Zed's shoulder was needling against the air force plane's leg as if he were tackling a dummy at football practice. Victor took a few more steps and turned around again.

This time, he saw several sets of eyeballs peeking out from behind the bushes around the airstrip. People began emerging, melting out of the woods and oozing onto the open strip of land to see what all the excitement was.

So much for secrecy. Victor adjusted his ski mask, which was making his face itch, and waved back to the locals who were gesturing to him from near the two planes. "Hi," he said, barely audible. "Don't mind us. Just some crazy white people wearing government-regulated wool ski masks in the equatorial heat, picking up a friend who has no first name and no last name."

Inside the hut, General Banja stood over FNU LNU, who had a bag over his head. Banja shook Victor's hand.

"My friend, once again I demonstrate to you Gabimbia's commitment to fighting terrorism. Here's everything he had with him when we picked him up." Banja handed Victor a bag.

"Washington appreciates your help, general."

Victor took FNU LNU by the arm and led him toward the door.

"I appreciate Washington! Do you see my new Range Rover?" General Banja called after Victor.

Victor saw the gleaming new SUV outside the door of the hut. "Nice color, general."

"Custom made!" Banja yelled. He clicked the key and the car made a happy beeping sound.

Victor led FNU LNU outside, back into the heavy heat that wouldn't break even for nighttime. Several Gabimbians were now helping Zed, still in his ski mask, and the pilot Roger to push the air force plane back a few inches. It had not been used since the last air show, almost a year ago, and its tires were flat, making it even more difficult to move. Victor stood back a few feet, watching, while FNU LNU stood by, silent, with a bag over his head. They remained that way for a solid minute, until at last the air force plane budged and Roger motioned to Victor to get back on the Learjet.

Zed was still thanking the local Gabimbians for their assistance moving the plane when Victor and FNU LNU reached the top of the stairs. His American accent was clear, even though he thanked them in their tribal tongue. They all wanted to shake Zed's hand, as if the masked man had done them a favor. Zed, sweat clearly visible at his armpits, his black ski mask stifling his breathing, was surrounded by eager Gabimbians. He pressed through the crowd to the stairs of the plane and bid them farewell. They stood huddled in a group while Roger maneuvered the plane around. As the jet took off, they melted back into the bush.

"That was certainly covert," Victor said to Zed once they were off the ground.

"We'll tweak it when we write the cable," Zed responded.

The two turned to look at FNU LNU, an unmoving lump that hadn't said a word. Zed pulled the bag off his head. The young man underneath looked at them, ambivalent. Victor opened the bag Banja had given him and sifted through papers that showed weather patterns, results from dirt sample tests, statistics on peanut consumption, and trajectories for marketing.

"What's your name?" Zed asked him.

"Gabriel Henna."

"You actually have a first and last name? Why didn't you answer the Gabimbian authorities when they asked you?"

"They never asked me anything. I arrived in Gabimbia last night for a meeting with a peanut farmer. I want to invest in his farm. Along the way to meet him, the police stop me, bring me to some military barracks, put a bag over my head, and now here I am."

"They never even questioned you?"

Victor groaned. Director was so ready to throw money to any ally willing to help Director's cause, the allies were now taking action, however false, just to get the money. Meanwhile, he knew, Omar al-Suqqit was planning a real attack. But Victor couldn't look for him, because he was sitting here with Gabriel Henna, a legitimate peanut investor who was taken in so Banja could get a new Range Rover.

Once back in Ajakar, they took Gabriel Henna to a safe house, where Victor made him a plate of pasta while Zed went to Station to talk to Director. He returned an hour later.

"Let's go. Roger's waiting for us."

Victor gave Zed a questioning look. Gabriel Henna looked up from the table but still said nothing.

"To go back to Gabimbia. Slight miscommunication from Director. We seem to have a case of mistaken identity here."

"What?" Victor said.

"We've got the wrong FNU LNU. Director wanted a FNU LNU in The Gambia picked up. Not Gabimbia. And they wanted Ahjak Station to do it, not Ajakar Station."

"How many FNU LNUs are going to get picked up because some munchkin thinks that's a real name?"

Zed motioned to Gabriel Henna to get up and before long they were all back on the Learjet, flying to Gabimbia again. They landed without incident this time, and Zed threw open the door and let down the stairs. He made a welcoming gesture to Gabriel, as if to say, "Please, after you," and Gabriel descended the stairs. He turned to look back up at Victor and Zed, as Zed pulled the stairs up and closed the door. Roger taxied back around for takeoff. Victor could see the locals coming out of the bushes again and Gabriel Henna, peanut investor, standing in the middle of the huddle, wondering what had just happened to him.

CHAPTER THIRTY-TWO
NUAKABATU, DEMOCRATIC REPUBLIC OF ZUZU

Omar stepped into the studio that Faruk had improvised in a shack that normally housed his brother's broom and mop shop. Faruk and Leyla were preparing to shoot her martyr video and, while Omar adored Leyla's enthusiasm, he knew she often needed to be kept on track. She had a tendency to let her mind wander and forget the task at hand, and this operation was too important to leave anything, including Leyla's attention, to chance.

The shack's cleaning tools were propped up in a corner and the counter had been cleared and covered with the Rubblestani flag. A map of Rubblestan was taped to the wall behind the counter. Three Kalashnikovs were propped up against the wall as decoration. Leyla sat on a stool in a corner, where a woman was making her up with mascara and blush. Faruk, still with his fez and clipboard, was ordering people around.

"Karim, we need another weapon in the shot!" He stopped when he saw Omar. "Omar!" He drew out the R sound for several seconds and gave Omar a hug. "Do you like?" he asked, gesturing to the scene he had created.

"Omar, I am so glad to see you," Leyla said through closed, unmoving lips, while the makeup woman applied lipstick.

"I won't disturb you. I just wanted to see how the video is coming along and make sure Leyla will be ready to leave with me tomorrow."

"You mustn't worry, my great emir," Faruk said. "We'll finish this afternoon." Leyla stood up and moved toward the background scenery.

Omar had sent for one of his lieutenants, who now entered the shack and stared, openmouthed, at Leyla, who was straddling a rocket-propelled grenade launcher. Omar called his name, twice, and the lieutenant finally turned to him.

"Sir?"

"I need you to run down to old Abdallah's place and see if he has ten vials of infectious bovine rhinotracheitis," Omar said. He was still annoyed that Core Central was wasting his time on such a task, so he had decided to assign it to an underling. "Tell Abdallah it's for me."

"Yes, emir. Shall I bring them here?"

"Bring them by the mailroom and we'll have them ship it off to Caliphate Crossing. In fact, before you run down there, see if you can get in touch with someone in Rubblestan and get the proper address to send the poison to. We wouldn't want it going to the wrong cave."

"Of course not, sir. No problem, sir." The lieutenant stole one last glance at Leyla then ran down the road to Abdallah's place.

CHAPTER THIRTY-THREE
AJAKAR, PIGALLO

Victor walked into Ajakar Station the following morning. Zed intercepted him before he could reach the shark tank.

"I know you won't bother reading the cable, but the counter-intelligence shop has put out some new regulations. You need to send them a list of all your Facebook friends."

Victor was annoyed. He hadn't had his morning caffeine yet. "First of all, why? Second of all, why don't they go to my Facebook page and look at the list if they're so concerned?"

"Relax. It's not just for you. It's for everyone. They want to trace every friend of every CYA employee and see if they can detect a pattern of foreign intel attempts to friend employees."

"Should make for a pretty big link chart in the end, if you believe the six degrees of separation theory."

"It will keep the CI shop busy. Go type up your list before Director sends me a friendly reminder."

"Come on. My mom is one of my Facebook friends. That's how menacing my friends are."

"An Italian who lives in France. The worst. A double threat."

Victor went to his desk. It occurred to him, as he logged on to his CYA computer, that he was still on the Terrorist Watch List himself. Yet, here he was, logging on to a highly classified system. He tried to scoot his chair down the desk to the unclassified system and realized he was on the GS-13 chair when it wobbled, squeaked, and nearly tipped him over. He pulled up *The New York Times* and the lead story immediately caught his attention: "President Authorizes Covert Action in Rubblestan." He read the article.

> "The president signed a presidential finding yesterday authorizing the CYA to conduct covert action in Rubblestan. The finding gives the CYA authority to implement its secret drone program and launch a clandestine war against the enemy."

How secret is it if it's on the front page of The New York Times? Victor wondered. He continued reading.

> "The CYA plans to deploy secret operatives to covert forward operating bases located throughout the country, including in the capital (see graphic). From these secret bases, the operatives will collect intelligence and orchestrate the covert program."

Victor looked at the caption for one of the photos, which showed a plane and a hangar with the backdrop of mountains. The caption read: "One of the hidden bases two miles east of Rubblestan's capital." Next to it were portrait photos of two men with big smiles. The caption read: "Bob Hardy and Tom Delaney, two of the CYA's secret operatives who are responsible for managing the Agency's clandestine drone program." There was also an interactive map of all covert forward operating bases in Rubblestan. Victor clicked on the link, which led him to a map listing each base's geo-coordinates. From there, he could click on any base for a 360-degree virtual tour and a detailed description of each base's function. *Maybe covert doesn't mean what I think it means,* Victor thought. He looked at a related story.

"United States government officials, who asked to remain anonymous for security reasons, today confirmed that David Rays is a covert agent working for the CYA and was in the process of collecting clandestine intelligence for the United States when he was arrested by Rubblestani authorities last week."

It's good the government officials asked to remain anonymous while outing a covert officer. Victor thought about all the officers in the CI shop who were perusing Facebook rather than looking for anonymous sources inside the government and shook his head. He heard a beep and looked on his classified computer monitor. Habibi was pinging him on his instant message.

HABIBI: I met with Akim last night. Writing up the cable now, but figured I'd share the info straight with you since God knows when this cable will actually make it out of coordination and get sent off into the main system. Suqqit's back in DRZ. He mentioned something about a video. And he's meeting with "the director." Akim didn't know what that meant, though.

VICTOR: Did you ask John Boy to run a search on the possible significance of "director"?

HABIBI: Can't get him to answer shit. He's probably on flextime. And he's moved to the IÜD's fusion center. Designed by Disney imagineers!

VICTOR: I don't get that place. What do they do that our analysts don't already do?

HABIBI: Drink coffee in a different building. They also have the most enormous TV screens you've ever seen.

VICTOR: How do I get a rotation there?

HABIBI: Are you a carbon-based, warm-blooded creature with a beating heart?

VICTOR: Yes.

HABIBI: Then I'm afraid you are overqualified. Go find Suqqit. I'll let you know if I get any more info on this end. But considering we're no longer doing ops, well, you can see my quandary.

VICTOR: Wait. What?

HABIBI: Thanks to the David Rays kerfuffle, no more ops.

VICTOR: So what are people like you doing there?

HABIBI: Paying off our mortgages. And watching a lot of movies.

VICTOR: Go find yourself a sheep.

HABIBI: Don't tempt me. Ciao.

***

Victor closed up his work area early and headed out to meet Axl Steiger for drinks at the Sofitel's pool bar. Director had told Victor to drop Axl as a potential source, but Victor knew his access to the Crown Prince's financial dealings was too precious to give up. When he had warned Zed he was going to meet Axl, Zed corrected him and said, "You are going to have dinner and wouldn't it be a funny coincidence if you happen to run into someone at the restaurant. Ajakar is a small town, after all."

Victor walked down the steps to the pool area and saw Axl at a table next to the ocean already sipping Johnnie Walker Blue.

"Victor, my friend. Do have a seat. Whiskey?" He gestured for Victor to sit down.

"Thank you, I never pass on Johnnie Blue."

"I haven't seen you around Ajakar for awhile. You weren't at the Ombudai National Day festivities last week."

"I was back in Washington for some training."

"You missed absolutely nothing, officially speaking. The most staid, sterile national day 'party.' Hell, they can't even call it a cocktail party. But the *after* party was something else. I've never seen so much alcohol. And the 'nieces'! Thank Allah for so many scantily clad nieces!" Axl downed what was left in his glass and poured some more. "The Crown Prince was there."

"Of Ombudai?" Victor asked.

"Yes. With a few of his nieces."

"He's pretty involved here in Pigallo now, isn't he?"

"That's why I have a job here. Between Pigallo and DRZ, that's a lot of his investments right now. He's been working with bin Fuqin in DRZ on a few construction projects. Here, it's mostly real estate."

"What do you think of the Crown Prince?" Victor asked him.

"Officially? A great man, doing his best to spread the wealth of his country and share his country's values with the masses."

"And unofficially?"

"The biggest fucking hypocrite I have ever seen. Living the dream in Marbella with his nieces in thong bikinis, while his subjects swelter in head-to-toe clothing in the fucking desert heat? Come on. And preaching against alcohol but loading his yacht with more whiskey than Johnnie Walker can shake his walking stick at?" He looked at his glass and took another sip. "He pays me to look the other way, so I do. It pays for a nice lifestyle, with my own nieces, if you know what I mean."

Victor took his own sip of Johnnie Walker and let it sit in his mouth for a few seconds, the heavy flavor encircling his teeth. Finally, he swallowed and said, "You know, there are people who would pay you *not* to look away."

"I've been coming to realize that," Axl said. "I imagine some people are quite interested in how the Crown Prince spends his time."

"And how he spends his money," Victor said. "Of course, you'd be in a position to know that, wouldn't you? Since you are his personal banker."

"These curious people, they might have something to offer in return?"

"I'd imagine they could keep your nieces well-adorned and entertained. In Ibiza, if you like. With champagne for lunch every day."

Axl looked out at the ocean. The moon reflected off the waves. He looked back at Victor. "I think I could do this."

CHAPTER THIRTY-FOUR
AJAKAR, PIGALLO

Victor went into the station the next day. Zed was in his office behind his desk, staring into a handheld mirror and scratching his face. He kept saying, "Fuck."

"What's the problem, chief?"

"That fucking mask gave me a rash. My skin is killing me." He put the mirror down. "What happened with our chocolate- and cheese-eating banker?"

"He's in."

"Holy Ricola! I knew it. It was the hypocrisy, wasn't it? He can't stand the hypocrisy. Good work, Victor." He scratched his face again and thought for a moment. "Here's what we're going to do. Nothing. We're not going to tell Director anything yet. Once we've got the goods, then we can figure out how to write it up. When are you seeing him again?"

"In two days."

"Good. Nothing till then, you understand me? Not a fucking word to any of those monkeys back in DC."

"Got it, chief."

"Now get the fuck out of here."

"Roger that." Victor went to his desk. He had a good case developing with Axl, but his mind was still on Omar and what he was planning next.

CHAPTER THIRTY-FIVE
NUAKABATU, DEMOCRATIC REPUBLIC OF ZUZU

Omar was packing his bags when his phone dinged. He was annoyed. He had enough to think about, what with packing for his move to Atlanta, organizing the acquisition of enough C-4 explosive and fertilizer to blow up the target, and keeping the hip-swaying Leyla on track to carry out her part of the mission, not to mention having to placate Core Central Leadership by purchasing a cow virus that had no chance of killing cows. It was Zawiki on instant message.

ZAWIKI: Did you make the purchase of the cow medicine?

OMAR: My lieutenant took care of it yesterday. It is being sent by courier.

ZAWIKI: Excellent work, Omar. I just wanted to wish you luck before your travels. We have an excellent trainee here who will be your main operational support person.

A trainee? Omar thought. *I am looking to blow up a major peanut refinery in the United States and Core Central assigns a trainee to provide me operational support?* Instead of voicing his frustration, Omar simply wrote: Appreciate that.

ZAWIKI: Trust you got the account info?

OMAR: Yes. Apartment rented. Tickets bought. Will be on the ground with the truck driver tomorrow.

ZAWIKI: Good luck.

CHAPTER THIRTY-SIX
AJAKAR, PIGALLO

Victor met Axl at a restaurant with a view over the city. Axl ordered schnitzel and Victor made a mental note to include this more-German-than-Swiss detail in his next cable to Director, a cable he knew he couldn't put off forever, especially if Axl actually delivered the goods.

After a few pleasantries, Axl slid an envelope across the table. Victor calmly but quickly placed it in his backpack.

"He's got investments all over, but mostly here in Pigallo and the DRZ. I think he's laundering through real estate in the DRZ, with some kickbacks going to bin Fuqin. I noted down a few other investments, including one that looks promising in France. A company called Pistache. It's got ties to a Malaysian company known to be involved in some shady business. I'll leave it to you to dig up the details." He stuck a huge piece of schnitzel in his mouth.

"You're doing the right thing," Victor told him.

"I'm not worried about that. I'm more worried about my favorite niece who's been threatening to leave me if I don't get her back to

Europe soon. Seems the smoke from burning trash here is bad for her skin. She's been begging for a spa treatment in Geneva."

Victor handed Axl a separate envelope, stuffed with cash. "This ought to make her happy then," he said.

Axl tucked the envelope in his inside jacket pocket. He finished his schnitzel, leaned back in his chair with a satisfied sigh, and said, "Pleasure doing business with you."

***

Now that the deed had been done with Axl Steiger, Zed and Victor knew they had to make Director aware of it on some level or the two of them could find themselves facing a Congressional panel at some point in the not so distant future.

"We'll finesse the cable. The hypocrisy of the Crown Prince made Axl feel he had no choice but to come to us with the info," Zed said. "Then we say that you will be traveling to Paris in order to approach the French to follow up on the company lead there. Maybe that will divert Director's focus from the fact that we disobeyed orders. I'll also throw in some crap about this being high on the threat matrix. That usually works."

***

Victor was preparing for his trip to Paris a few days later when Zed walked into the shark tank. "Director didn't like our finessed cable."

"Details on the Crown Prince's financials didn't make up for it?" Victor asked.

"Apparently info on a prince possibly supporting terrorism is not a priority when said prince is considered a good friend by many in Washington. Director also quashed your trip to France.

Don't take that part personally. Nobody in Washington likes to work with the French."

"So that's it? We just stop working?"

"Director has a huge backlog of FNU LNU traces they'd like help with."

Victor dropped his head down on the desk and his arms flopped out on either side. He began moaning.

"Head up, Caro."

Victor lolled his head to the side so he could prop his chin on the desk. He stared past Zed, looking as if his soul had left him and his body was just a bag of air.

"Fuck 'em all," Zed said. "Autistic monkeys with no thumbs contribute more to society, but we're stuck with Director."

Victor moaned again.

"Doesn't your mother live in Paris?"

Victor stared lifelessly at Zed.

"Maybe you need a break to go visit her."

Victor's eyes registered something.

"Who knows who else you might run into in Paris. You've got some old friends there, right?"

Victor sat up and looked straight ahead of him. He did have friends in Paris, friends who worked for the French intelligence service, with whom he had carried out a joint operation several years before.

"I'm still on the Terrorist Watch List. Victor Caro can't fly. With the biometrics they have at Charles de Gaulle airport, I can't enter as Stan Moakley. They already have me tagged as Victor Caro."

"I'll handle it. You just plan your trip." Zed left the shark tank and slammed the door to his office.

Victor pulled up his instant messaging system and pinged Taylor, another training classmate, who, Victor had heard through the rumor channels, had recently been assigned to Paris.

VICTOR: Hey, Taylor. Congratulations on Paris. I didn't realize you speak French.

TAYLOR: Hey, man! Thanks, but I don't speak French. I was studying Japanese, remember? Paul from training, he's a native French speaker. But he's taking a remedial English course so couldn't come. Director won't let him go overseas until he speaks English. They needed someone immediately to fill in for an officer who had to cancel his tour at the last minute when his dog got diagnosed with some awful dog disease. The guy wrote all about his ordeal in the pet database at Director.

VICTOR: Listen, I'm coming your way.

TAYLOR: Great! I could use some socializing with someone I know. I find it hard to meet the locals since I don't speak French.

VICTOR: Did you see the cable about the finances of the Crown Prince of Ombudai?

TAYLOR: I saw it. Interesting. Sorry we aren't allowed to do much from here.

VICTOR: No worries. But maybe we can catch up over coffee? I'm coming to Paris to visit my mother.

TAYLOR: Sure.

VICTOR: Great. I'll be in touch once I know my schedule.
Till then....

Zed came back to Victor's desk. "I fixed your Terrorist Watch List problem. Just don't ever change your last name to Q-U-apostrophe-A-R-O. And maybe don't spell Victor with a K."

"You couldn't just say, 'Take Victor Caro off the list'?"

"First, that wouldn't be any fun at all. Second, removing a name from the list requires that person to prove he or she is not a terrorist."

"How does one prove one is not a terrorist?"

"Exactly. This is why no one has ever been able to remove his name from the list. Changing the spelling can be done by professional terrorist hunters like us, in order to avoid another debacle like the underwear bomber. We had his name, we just spelled it wrong. Besides, what's one more name on that list? Senator Kennedy was on that list. Probably still is. Now go get packed. You're going to Paris, remember?"

CHAPTER THIRTY-SEVEN
PARIS

Victor stepped off the plane in Paris and welcomed the sight of a bustling city that kept stray dogs at bay and whose residents did not burn trash or urinate in public. He didn't mind these things in Ajakar—it was part of that city's ironic charm—but Paris was a nice break from the chaos of Africa.

He took a taxi into town, made a quick phone call to his old friend, then took another taxi to his mother's apartment.

Giulia was a native Italian who had married a French-American man, Olivier, who had gone to Bologna, Italy, in the sixties to study at the university there and who soon embraced the city's communist leanings. When Giulia became pregnant, they quickly married and Victor's mother helped Olivier come to the realization that it was probably best for him to stop smoking hashish every night at the local Red Brigade bar and to get a job to support their new family.

As an engineer, much to his Red Brigade colleagues' chagrin, Olivier easily landed a job at the Ferrari factory just outside of Bologna. Within a couple of years, the previously populist Olivier had become quite wealthy and readjusted his ideological outlook.

After Ferrari won Imola two years running, thanks to Olivier's engineering brilliance, Olivier fully ensconced himself in the capitalist system and eventually moved his family to Paris's chic sixteenth *arrondissement*, a bastion of the bourgeoisie on the city's west side.

"Why are you so skinny?" Giulia asked Victor. "Don't you eat? Or are you starving like all the Africans now?"

"That's racist, Mom."

"It's only racist if it's not true. Look at you. Bones. Come in and eat."

Victor admittedly relished his mother's cooking, but as he shoveled tortellini into his mouth, his mother's staring at him put him off.

"What is it, Ma?"

"Nothing. I'm not even going to ask. It's none of my business." She was haughty.

"Ma, what?"

"No, forget it. I'm not going to ask about your work. You can't tell me, so I won't even ask. It's better that way. I don't know what to tell people when they ask, but that's all right. I'll just look like a mother who doesn't know her own child." She had left Italy, but she had retained her Italian skill for making others feel guilty.

Victor sighed and put down his fork. He rued the day he had told his mother the truth. She had been so proud when he told her he had taken the Foreign Service exam and been accepted into the United States diplomatic corps. She and Victor's father, who was half American, had instilled in Victor that the United States was the Land of Opportunity, and they consistently encouraged him to make a life for himself there. Now, he was representing his great country. She told all her friends he would be ambassador one day. Six years later, Victor was tired of lying to his own mother and broke down one night and told her the truth. Giulia considered his real profession sleazy and compared it to a used car salesman. Victor had to admit, she was right on both counts. But he was very good at it, and wasn't sleaze a virtue when it was done to serve one's country?

"Ma, we've been through this. Tell your friends I work at the embassy. Everybody's work there is classified, so it's normal you don't know any details."

"You disappear. I didn't hear from you for two weeks that time. I was so worried."

"I can't always contact you when I'm traveling. You know that."

"Not even your own mother?"

"No, Ma. Not even you."

"I don't know. Anne-Marie was talking the other day at lunch about her son Jean. He's a doctor, you know. On and on she went, about how he saves babies. But I couldn't say anything about my son."

"All right, Mom. Enough. I need to go. I'm meeting a friend."

"Don't tell me! I don't want to know any more!"

Victor stood up and kissed her on the cheek. "I'll see you later, Ma."

***

Robert was a distinguished silhouette sitting at a back table at the café in Rue de Frederique. The smoke from his cigarette swirled as he sipped an espresso. He and Victor had worked together on an operation in Beirut that had involved an Iranian arms shipment to Hezbollah. Director had deemed the operation too risky, but when the French decided to go ahead—with or without their American counterpart—Director grudgingly gave Victor the go ahead, figuring if the operation failed, the French could take the blame, and if it succeeded, the CYA would be redeemed for past failures. The operation succeeded, but the White House blocked Director from touting the achievement, fearing the president might suffer in the polls if he was seen to be cooperating with the French.

"It's been a long time, Victor." Robert's accent was thick, his voice deep. "I don't think we said a proper goodbye in Beirut." They shook hands.

"You disappeared too fast, and I had a boat to catch." Victor sat down.

"It was fun, though, no?"

"The most fun I've ever had with a wig and a gun."

"I've had some other fun with a wig and a gun, but never mind that." Robert laughed and took a long drag on his cigarette. "Tell me, what brings you to Paris?"

"I'm visiting my mother."

"Of course you are. And you happened to run into me. So?"

Victor explained to Robert the information he had gotten from Axl Steiger. "I need as much information on Pistache as possible. What are their financial dealings? Who do they buy from? Sell to? Who works for them? Everything. Our intel shows the company they work with in Malaysia has direct ties to the Core."

Robert exhaled a ring of smoke. It floated in the air for a few seconds before dissipating. He tapped the cigarette's ashes into an ashtray and took another sip of coffee. "You know I left the service last year. *Directeur* and I had a slight disagreement when they offered the top operational job to a *monsieur* who has never recruited a proper source. With one exception." He looked directly at Victor and blew smoke in his face. "An Arab camel trainer, who made up some *merde* about a terrorist plotting to poison the camel food supply chain. He failed to mention that the man he was accusing was also his country's top camel breeder who had refused to sell his strongest male to the camel trainer. We planted unmentionable stories about the breeder. It was a huge scandal in the camel racing world."

"That was you guys?"

"Unfortunately, yes. All the while, *Directeur* was feeding this source thousands of euros. He built a new lap pool to train his racing camels, courtesy of the French Intelligence Service." He took another long drag on his cigarette. "Did you know camels swim in lap pools to train for races? It's very funny to watch."

"You still have connections though?" Victor asked.

Robert nodded. "I can get this information on your company. It will be between us, if you don't mind. If *Directeur* finds out, I could lose my head." He tapped his cigarette on the ashtray. "We actually did that here, you know, making people lose their heads. Perhaps you can, how do you say, make it worth my while?"

"The usual?"

"Please, yes."

"Good to know you still have impeccable taste, Robert."

***

They met the next day in the Tuileries Garden and strolled through the trees and around a pond.

"It is an interesting company, this Pistache." Robert had an unlit cigarette dangling from his lips. "They export nuts. Oddly, one of the places they export to is the Democratic Republic of Zuzu, which as you know is one of the world's largest producers of nuts. So why is the DRZ importing nuts from France?"

"The Crown Prince has several business interests in the DRZ and we think he's feeding bin Fuqin's coffers."

"Interestingly, Pistache just opened a new branch." He stopped walking and lit his cigarette. "In the United States." He took a long puff and started walking again. "Atlanta."

The capital of America's top peanut producing state and home to dozens of peanut refineries, thought Victor. It made sense.

Robert handed Victor a dossier. "Here's everything I found."

Victor took the dossier and swung his backpack off his back.

"And now, you have something for me, no?"

Victor tucked the dossier into his backpack and pulled out a plastic squeeze bottle of French's mustard. Robert made a sound like a man pining for a beautiful woman who has just entered a room.

"You come from the land of Dijon, but you want French's mustard, made in the USA. I'll never understand it."

"It is the best for hamburgers." He dropped the *H* sound, so it sounded like *amburgers.*

Victor shook his head and maneuvered his backpack over his shoulder. "Thank you, Robert. This time, we can shake hands goodbye."

"No, my friend. For French's, I kiss you." Robert grabbed Victor's shoulders and pulled him close, kissing first one cheek and then the other. "We will see each other again." Robert walked behind a tree and melted away.

***

"Sorry I'm late!" Taylor jaunted up to Victor at a sidewalk kiosk, where Victor was shuffling through out-of-print books. "I lost track of time at the studio."

"The studio?"

"I'm a model for a nude drawing class. I like to really get to know a culture when I live in it."

They walked down to the river together. "Listen, Taylor, I've got a small world story for you. I just happened to run into an old friend here. A friend with connections. Who happened to know a lot about Pistache. And who happened to give me this dossier."

Taylor looked at the envelope stuffed with papers. "That *is* a small world story."

"I'm visiting my mom here. I'm not working. But this seems like it might be relevant information."

Taylor was peeking inside.

"Maybe someone walked in to the embassy and gave you that."

"People walk in with information all the time."

"Maybe Paris Station finds it relevant enough to send to Director."

"That might happen."

"You'd have to send a copy to Ajakar, given the subject matter."

"Of course," Taylor agreed.

They smiled at each other and shook hands.

***

"That was a quick trip." Giulia was standing in the doorway to Victor's room, her arms crossed as she leaned on the doorjamb.

"It was an unofficial, non-working work trip. But I have to get back to Ajakar. I've got some projects that need my attention."

She put her hand up to stop him. "Don't tell me. The less I know, the better. Here, take this." She handed him two packages of Camembert cheese and thick Italian salami. "I know they don't have food there. This will keep you from starving, for a little while at least."

"Thanks, Ma. They do have food there, but it's not as good as this." He put the food into his luggage, along with some other amenities he had picked up to bring back, like sunscreen and new T-shirts that didn't have sweat stains in the armpits. He stood up and grabbed his bag. "I'll call you when I land."

"One time you can call, another time you can't. I don't understand this sneaking around you do."

He leaned over and gave her a peck on the cheek. "Love ya, Ma. Don't change." He hauled his suitcase down to the street and hailed a taxi to the airport.

CHAPTER THIRTY-EIGHT
NUAKABATU, DEMOCRATIC REPUBLIC OF ZUZU

O mar and Leyla arrived four hours early for their 1 a.m. flight to Paris, where they would catch an onward flight to Atlanta. Zuzuans crowded the airline desk, a bubbling mass of sweaty flesh pushing and squeezing in the humid nighttime heat, eager to embark on the city's only weekly flight to Paris. Most carried little or no luggage, saving their allotted weight for the return trip, when they would be laden down with toasters, televisions, and other consumer goods purchased in Europe.

At the desk, the airline employee handed Omar and Leyla hand-written tickets. They were about to move away from the desk when she grabbed them back, stamped them six times each with a unicorn stamp, then returned them to Omar and Leyla with a smile.

They went next to the security line, which was not a line at all but, like at the airline desk, more of a huddle of people squeezing through the metal detector machine with their carry-on luggage. The machine stood alone, with no gates or other security apparatus around it. One could have easily stepped around it and into the terminal. But Zuzuans were honest people and pushed ahead until they wedged themselves through its lonely arch. The machine beeped continuously, but the soldier manning it was on a cigarette break in the corner.

Once on the plane, Omar watched Leyla as she removed a bright pink neck support pillow from her bag. She draped it across her long neck, a delicate smile dancing on her lips. Omar got one last whiff of the heavy Nuakabatu air before the flight attendant closed the airplane door and, as though she were whipping pistols out of a holster, flicked off the tops of two cans of anti-mosquito spray, which she released in a long hiss down the entire length of the plane.

They arrived in Paris as the sun was coming up. Leyla was groggy and temperamental, rolling her pink bag with a pout on her face. Omar was awake, aware of the clanking of the luggage cart on the tarmac, the whir of the engines as they slowed, the hum of the bus that carried them from the plane to the terminal. He felt alive and in perpetual motion, moving always forward toward his operation.

Because their next flight was going to the United States, they had to check in and go through security a second time. Omar felt inconvenienced by this, but also a little proud. The Core had managed to change the entire way airports operated.

Leyla went ahead of Omar in the line and he watched the small sway of her hips as she approached the counter, just as another desk opened and a woman called out, "Next!" Omar stepped up to the desk.

"Welcome to USA Air, sir. What is your final destination and may I see your passport, please?"

Omar handed the plucky airline employee his passport and said, "Good morning, miss. I am going to Atlanta. May I say, what a beautiful smile you have."

"Why, thank you!" she said, drawing out her southern drawl ' and giggling just slightly. She typed spiritedly on her computer, paused for a moment, confused, and then typed in the information again. "Isn't that strange," she said. "I see the problem." She typed some more and the printer made its familiar printing sound and spit out a boarding pass. As she gathered all of his papers together, she said to Omar, "You won't believe this. There's an Umar Sukkit on the Terrorist Watch List."

"No!" Omar said, feigning shock.

"Yes," she said with wide eyes and a few bouncing nods of her head. "Clearly that's not you, since your name is spelled differently. I'm so sorry for the inconvenience, Mr. al-Suqqit, and for any offense that may have caused. Hang on." She went back to her keyboard and the printer spit out another piece of paper. "I've upgraded you," she said with a wink. "Please feel free to visit our VIP lounge in the terminal for a foot massage. Again, please accept our apologies."

"Not to worry, miss. Thank you so much for your help." He took his papers and walked over to Leyla, who was waiting on the side.

They moved on to the security line where hundreds—maybe thousands?—of people waited, patiently or impatiently, in a line that snaked through a maze of barriers. Now Omar felt truly inconvenienced. He knew it was an unintended consequence of his brothers' actions, but still, he couldn't help feeling annoyed. He took a deep breath and got in line with Leyla, who watched the video about how to take her shoes off four times and who stared with admiration at the new bright blue uniforms of the transportation security officers, as though entranced by their crispness.

Omar approached the X-ray machine and easily slid out of his slip-on shoes, which he had worn specifically so he wouldn't hold up the security line, since that can be so embarrassing. He saw Leyla pull out a giant cosmetics bag while he placed his plastic baggie with his hand sanitizer in a bin. He walked through the metal detector.

"Sir, is this your baggie?" One of the security officers in a bright blue uniform called Omar over.

Omar walked over to him and realized he was standing right next to a most wanted poster with his own portrait on it. He was thrilled he was wanted internationally, as any Core emir would be, but he was also self-conscious, noting how old the photo was and how the unflattering angle and terrible lighting made him look like an unkempt Muppet.

"Yes, that's my baggie," Omar said.

The officer held up Omar's bottle of hand sanitizer. "This is a three-and-a-half-ounce bottle. You're only allowed three point four ounces."

"Here is where I always get confused," Omar said to the officer while still standing next to his most wanted picture. "The bottle itself is three-and-a-half ounces, but it is only half full, so I have less than three point four ounces of hand sanitizer."

"I'll let it go, sir," he said to Omar with a wink. "I'm kind of a germaphobe myself. But please remember for next time. Do you mind if take a drop?"

"Please," Omar said. The officer squeezed out some hand sanitizer and cleaned his hands. Omar waited patiently, observing the poster of himself and making a mental note to get an updated portrait made once he was back home. Perhaps he'd get a picture of himself holding a kitten or a goat. The officer handed back the bottle with a smile. "Enjoy your trip, sir."

CHAPTER THIRTY-NINE
AJAKAR, PIGALLO

At the airport in Ajakar, Victor ran his hands through his sweaty hair and grabbed his bag off the carousel. An officer was circling amongst the luggage with a sniffing dog. Victor took a deep breath, letting the heat fill his lungs until they burned and trying to discern the different odors that instantly brought him back to Pigallo. No other place smelled like this, like raw sewage thrown on top of a burning pile of trash that has been vomited on and that has a family of goats living around it. He was home.

Sitting at the immigration desk was Babaka, his eyes big and bright behind his thick glasses. He never stopped smiling. "Mister Caro!" He beamed at Victor and opened his arms wide and motioned to Victor to come toward him. "Come, Mister Caro! I am so pleased to see you! I was so happy to hear you decided not to be a terrorist! We got a memo from your embassy telling us you are not a bad guy after all. This is a very wise choice, Mr. Caro."

"Thank you, Babaka."

Victor placed his passport on the table. He was about to speak when the sniffing dog surprised him with a loud yelp right next to his luggage. The officer tried to move on but the dog was insistent, barking ferociously at Victor's bag.

"What is it, Alkaseltzer?" Babaka said to the dog. The other officer calmed the dog down.

"His name is Alkaseltzer?" Victor asked.

"Yes. Alkaseltzer. I once see this name in a newspaper you give me, Mr. Caro. And I think, what a beautiful name! So I give this name to the dog."

The officer said to Victor, "I need to search your bag, sir."

Victor hoisted the bag onto the table and unzipped it. The powerful stench of fermenting milk exploded like a thunderclap the moment Victor opened the luggage. Alkaseltzer began barking again. The officer reached into the bag and pulled out the two packages of Camembert cheese. He looked at Victor and asked, "What is this?"

"Cheese."

"What is in the cheese?"

"Raw milk and probably some bacteria."

"Did you know drug cartels have started using cheese to cover the smell of drugs they are trafficking?" the officer asked Victor.

"I was not aware of that, sir. But that," he said pointing to the Camembert, "is just cheese."

Babaka's smile had disappeared. "You give up being a terrorist to start trafficking drugs? This is so disappointing, Mr. Caro."

The officer deliberately unwrapped the two packets of cheese and laid them on the table. He contemplated each one, moving around the table to see the cheeses from all perspectives. He raised a hand above his head, still staring at the cheese, then brought the side of his open hand down to chop into one of the rounds of the bacterial bastion that is Camembert. He chopped his hand throughout the oozing cheese, through the middle and along the sides, looking for drugs. Soon the Camembert was an exploded, stinking mess of rubbery goo. He repeated the process on the other cheese round.

"No drugs," the officer said.

"Oh, Mr. Caro!" Babaka was smiling again. "I am so pleased we do not have to arrest you!" He stamped Victor's passport five times and signed his name on each stamp. "Welcome home, Mr. Caro!"

CHAPTER FORTY
SOMEWHERE OVER THE ATLANTIC OCEAN

Omar looked across the first class cabin at Leyla. She had reclined her seat and drifted off while paging through Cosmopolitan magazine. She looked peaceful, her fuchsia skirt draped across her fit legs, outlining their shapeliness. The skirt was pulled up just the slightest bit to reveal her sparkly anklet, which tinkled each time she so much as twitched. Her painted toes peeked out from her sparkly sandals.

On his other side was a hefty man whom Omar assumed was an air marshal, since he had seen him whispering with a flight attendant before takeoff. He was reading a book called, "*Irrational Killers: Faith, Murder, and the Psychology of Jihad.*" He had it open on his lap and Omar could see he was diligently highlighting important passages, such as, "Even in the year AD 630, Mohammed despised America and freedom." Omar ordered a whiskey, believing he would be forgiven for such an act under these circumstances, and adjusted his American flag lapel pin, which the air marshal had noticed and given a nod of appreciation, as if to say, "That pin puts us on the same side, brother." Omar was pleased it seemed to divert the air marshal from realizing that Omar resided atop the FBI's Most Wanted List. Omar relished the alcohol as it burned his throat. He leaned back and settled in for the long flight.

CHAPTER FORTY-ONE
AJAKAR, PIGALLO

Victor arrived back at Ajakar Station and went straight to Zed's office. The chief was staring intently at his computer screen and running a finger down the left side of the text. He typed another sentence and then turned to Victor with a broad grin. Victor gave him a questioning look.

"If you read the first letter of each line of my cable," he said, "it spells Copernicus."

"And you're pleased with yourself." Victor sat down. "Did Taylor write it up as a walk-in to Embassy Paris?"

"Yep. He included all the info. Pistache's being linked to the Crown Prince and funneling money to Pigallo and the DRZ. But Director said to drop it, said it got zero hits when it traced Pistache. You'll hate me for this, but you better check in with John Boy and double check. Zero hits is weird, even for Director."

Victor went to the shark tank and pulled up a chat window to ping John Boy, who gave Victor an enthusiastic greeting before launching into a soliloquy on the genius of imagineers and bragging about having three monitors for his computer. Victor brought him back to the matter at hand.

VICTOR: I was wondering if you saw the info about Pistache, a French front company laundering money in Pigallo and DRZ and which just opened a branch in Atlanta.

JOHN BOY: Afraid I didn't see that one. I haven't had much time to read the cables coming in. I've been reworking the colors for the threat level chart.

VICTOR: Director said there were no hits.

JOHN BOY: Then it must not be a bad company. Otherwise we would know.

VICTOR: It is a bad company. I've got evidence linking it to laundering and terrorists.

JOHN BOY: I'm afraid that's not possible. Because then that information would have turned up when the company was traced.

VICTOR: It wouldn't have, because this is new information.

JOHN BOY: If your information doesn't support what we already know, it's probably not good information.

VICTOR: But we didn't know anything before. This information suggests it is a company that is up to no good.

JOHN BOY: If the company is doing bad things, then we should already know about it. Instead, it turned up no hits, so it must be fine.

Victor took a deep breath before responding again.

VICTOR: All I'm saying is, I have a hard time believing we have no information whatsoever on this company.

JOHN BOY: Didn't you just say you have information?

VICTOR: Other information. I can't believe we don't have other information about this company. We get hits on every company we ever trace; even if they're not derogatory hits, at least we know the name of the company and know it exists. And Pistache, nothing? Not a single shred of information?

JOHN BOY: Let me do a quick search.

His instant message cursor blinked in place for a few seconds.

JOHN BOY: I found something! A cable from Paris, just the other day.

VICTOR: That's the cable with my information in it.

JOHN BOY: At least next time someone requests traces, we know there will be some information for them! That's good news.

VICTOR: Thanks for all your help, John Boy.

JOHN BOY: Thanks, Victor. Let me know if I can help with anything else!

CHAPTER FORTY-TWO
ATLANTA

Omar and Leyla stepped off the plane in Atlanta and felt a burst of humid hot air until they made it safely into the air-conditioned terminal. They stood in the long line to have their passports checked. Omar was nervous. His passport was real but the visa was fake and had been put together hastily by the document forger with the lowest bid. Leyla was calm—her visa was real—and she was humming Britney Spears quietly and dancing a little in place.

When Omar was next in line, a small commotion broke out in front of him.

"What do you mean I have to go to secondary?" a man was saying to the passport control officer. He was clearly angry.

"Sir, just stay calm. They will ask you a few more questions in there," the officer said to the man while pointing to the room where immigration officers grilled people with questionable passports, visas, or stories for coming to America.

"Why are you sending me there? I'm an American citizen."

"Standard procedure, sir. Anyone who has traveled to Rubblestan gets sent to secondary."

"I went to Rubblestan for the government of the United States. I shouldn't be sent to secondary."

The officer was trying to remain calm. "What do you do for the government of the United States?"

The man held up his passport. Across the front in large gold letters was written DIPLOMATIC PASSPORT.

"Take a wild fucking guess what I do for the USG."

"There's no need for strong language, sir. It is standard procedure that anyone who has traveled to Rubblestan goes to secondary for additional questioning."

"I go to that shithole as a representative of the United States government—who you work for, too, by the way; you and I work for the same government—and my reward for getting shot at with mortars and trying to negotiate a peace deal is to not be allowed back into my own country, the very same country that sent me to the shithole in the first place. Is that what you're telling me?"

Another officer had come to the desk during the man's rant and began forcing him toward the holding room. He was still yelling, "I go to a war zone to protect other people's freedom, and I'm not even free in my own country!"

Omar watched as the man was dragged away. He was glad that the Core had worked out a system with the Rubblestani authorities not to stamp the passports of Core fighters, thus concealing how many times the fighters had been in and out of Rubblestan. He cleared his throat as he approached the passport control officer, who was shaking his head and looking exasperated.

"You would think if he really worked for the government he would know the regulations," the officer said to Omar, taking his passport with hardly a glance at his face. "Then nice people like you come from halfway around the world, looking for better opportunities, and you have to see that," he motioned with his head to the secondary room, where the man was now sitting with his elbows on his knees, his head in his hands. "I'm sorry you had to witness that." He stamped Omar's passport and said with a gentle smile, "Welcome to the United States of America!"

CHAPTER FORTY-THREE
AJAKAR, PIGALLO

The gray clouds were threatening to burst and break the afternoon heat, so Zed and Victor chose a table on the restaurant's veranda. Bright bougainvillea climbed the walls, covering the chipping paint with spurts of orange and pink flowers. A mangy dog paced back and forth in the road, where young children in dirty clothes held up boxes filled with gum and cigarettes, gaining the attention of passers-by, while their younger siblings stealthily picked their pockets. Many of Ajakar's businessmen were having lunch, some dressed in western business suits, others in the traditional dashiki. Zed and Victor ordered bottled water and beer, which Zed suggested they both needed to get through the rest of the day.

"You're going to have to go back, you know," Zed said. "It doesn't make any sense. Even for Director, it's too far-fetched this company doesn't exist in some database. If this Pistache is sending money to the States, and if al-Suqqit is planning something there, and the two are connected, we'll be the ones taking the fall, even though Director says there's nothing to it. Do you have any contacts at the FBI?"

"I do," Victor said, blowing away the foam on his beer. "She and I worked together on a case in Boston a few years back. I had a Libyan I was following who was trying to buy some restricted technology from a company up there. She helped set the company up to sell the parts to the guy, but slipped in a beacon so we could track it all."

"And?"

"One of the middlemen was a US citizen. Didn't know he was in the middle of some sticky shit. He's probably cleaning toilets in a federal prison in Massachusetts."

"And your Libyan?"

"He was involved in acquiring all kinds of bad shit for their weapons program. Once they knew we knew who he was, the guy was pretty limited in what he could do. Anyway, Vanessa was a major player in the case."

Their food arrived and they dug into their sandwiches.

"We need to get you back to Washington," Zed said. "You need to meet with her off-line. See if there's more to this. Is Director dicking us around, or are they really clueless?"

"Do you really want me to answer that?"

"Fuck it. Both answers suck. Request 'consultations.' They love that."

Victor groaned.

"I know it's a bitch," Zed said, "but it will get you back to Washington. Just make sure you don't say consultations for a case. They'll think it means they have to work and they won't approve the travel. Make it something innocuous, like you want to discuss your career path and where you're going next. They love that shit. Then while you're back, go visit Vanessa. See if she can dig up any more info on Pistache from her side."

A few days later, after several emails and cables to justify his trip and gather all the needed authorizations, Victor was back on a plane heading for Washington.

CHAPTER FORTY-FOUR
ATLANTA

The beige carpet was new and Omar walked around on it in his bare feet, feeling the fibers squish between his toes. He took in every detail of his new apartment, the white walls, the dark brown cupboards, the yellow linoleum in the kitchen, which was cold under his feet. He opened the refrigerator door and guffawed at how cold and big it was. He shared a small square refrigerator with a few of his lieutenants back in the DRZ, but generally they ate what they had each day. The fridge was reserved for specialty items, the occasional bottle of camel milk and such. Omar opened the other side of the refrigerator and was nearly knocked backwards by the freezing cold that escaped. Up in a corner he saw a plastic container full of strange oblong objects. He touched one. It stuck to his fingers. He brought it close to his face and examined it, amazed. He could not believe that he had his own ice cube maker.

He went to the sink to shake the ice cube off his finger and saw, to his right, a white metal door with a few dings here and there, a knob, and a handle. He pushed the handle and the door popped open. Inside were two plastic drawers. *How wonderful to have drawers for my clothes!* He pulled out a plastic basket that fit into the lower drawer. *Look! A shower caddy for all my shaving needs. These Americans have thought of everything!*

He walked to the living room window, which looked out onto an alley lined with two large dumpsters. He saw a young couple in leather jackets with their arms around each other, strolling through the narrow road. He could see Leyla's building a few streets down. She was back at work at the refinery and conducting the last bits of reconnaissance they would need for their plan. He turned back to his empty living room. He made a mental note to ask the rental office about his dishwasher. Omar had not seen her anywhere.

He glanced down at his *shalwar kameez* then surveyed his empty apartment. He was accustomed to his flowing clothes and sitting on the floor, but he recognized that, if he was going to fit in here in Atlanta, he needed new clothes and new furniture. It was time for a makeover.

CHAPTER FORTY-FIVE
WASHINGTON, DC

The glass façade drained Victor's energy the moment he saw it. He took a deep breath to prepare himself, to force himself to stay calm, and he passed through the turnstiles and returned to the stale air environment of Director. He walked across the great seal and past the Agency's motto engraved on the wall, "The truth shall make you free." *But it won't get you promoted,* Victor thought.

He walked into the Africa Department's front office, where Kinesha now sat as a gatekeeper. She had framed a new photo of her cats and painted her long fingernails yellow, green, red, and black.

"Good to see you, Kinesha. You're looking well, as are your cats." Victor picked up the photo.

Kinesha's furrowed brow softened and her face lit up. "Why, thank you!" she said with a big smile. "What can I help you with today?"

"I have consultations with the chief of the department. I believe our meeting was scheduled for noon."

She tilted her head slightly, gave Victor a sidelong glance, and smiled flirtatiously. "Just let me look here on the calendar. Are you Victor Caro?"

"I am."

She looked at him as if she was trying to remember where she had seen him before, but she couldn't quite place him. "Jim will be with you in a few minutes. Have a seat."

Victor sat down and scanned the outer office. Brightly colored African print textiles were hanging on the walls, many with the faces of various African presidents printed on them. A large wooden hippo sat in a corner. A fertility mask, painted green and blue, was propped on a bookshelf. He realized people brought back the best of Africa as souvenirs for life. But the smells, the sights, the gritty feel could not be shoved in a suitcase and displayed forever as a memory. Although malaria was pretty easy to bring back and keep for life, he realized.

Jim called Victor into his office. The new department chief had served in South Africa once years ago, but left before his tour was up, citing security concerns related to his family. "Security concerns" was one of those buzz phrases that made Director anxious. Including the phrase in a cable almost certainly assured an officer's request would be granted, because Director never wanted its Legal Department to have to explain to Congress that a security concern was left unaddressed. It turned out, however, that Jim's "security concerns" were related to his wife's banging a Rhodesian diamond dealer while Jim was at the office pushing electronic paper every day. He and his family returned to Washington and never went overseas again. Because Jim had spent so much time at Director, he had networked his way to the top.

"Good to see you, Victor," he said. "Looks like you've done a lot of chasing ghosts." He snickered as if he had said something funny.

"FNU LNU was a massive snafu," Victor said.

"FNU LNU? That's serious stuff. I'm talking about Omar al-Suqqit. Why waste your time? A guy like that can hardly operate in such a backwards country. He's neutralized."

Victor responded in a serious tone, "I think the Brotherhood is up to something, sir. I'm not ready to give up quite yet."

"I admire your perseverance. It won't get you anywhere, but I admire it."

Victor tried to smile but found it difficult.

"I understand you came back to consult about your next steps, career-wise."

Victor resented this charade. If he had cared about money, he would have become a banker. If he had cared about power, he would have aimed for CEO at a Fortune 500 company. He cared about mission, doing the right thing for his country, no matter how pansy that sounded. How could he explain to the department chief that he didn't give a rat's ass about promotion and had fabricated the need for consultations just so he could get back to Washington to secretly meet with a friend at the FBI to try to figure out what a terrorist and his financier were up to because Director seemed determined not to care? The department chief would crush him for not being concerned with his career trajectory. He was lying to his employer in order to do his job, while his employer chastised him for not caring about his job. Rather than launch into a tirade about the irony, Victor simply smiled.

"I'm afraid it's bad news for you, Victor. I don't see Rubblestan on your resume. I mean, you've gone there, but only on temporary duty. You haven't been posted there. Enjoying the garden spots of Africa instead."

The stench of Ajakar came to Victor's mind, along with a mental image of the kid who slept with a goat on Victor's street and who had lice crawling on his head and whose father attached flip-flops to his own hands in order to drag himself around since his legs had shriveled from polio, the vaccine for which had rotted in the village medical clinic because there was no electricity to keep the refrigerator running. It wasn't exactly a garden spot, but he didn't try to explain that to a man whose only experience in Africa was in a fancy compound in Pretoria, living next door to a rich Rhodesian diamond dealer.

"If you want a promotion, you go to Rubblestan. Look, I know, you watch a lot of movies, but we gotta tell Congress we flooded the place. Otherwise they think we're not taking this whole war seriously. We just built an enormous embassy there. How will it look if we don't fill it with people? I mean, I know those people can't actually go out and meet locals and do their jobs. It's much too dangerous for that. But we have to fill the building. We built an Olympic-sized pool, for Christ's sake! Someone has to use it so this won't have been a waste of taxpayers' dollars. And the fact that we keep sending people there lets the American people know we're winning. Your other option is to fill one of these 'corporate' slots. Like, head of the trainees. Passing on your knowledge to the next generation. Teach them how to write a cable. Take a leadership course. That's how you get promoted. What have you been doing? Hiding out in the field for ten years recruiting people? How do you think that looks to the promotion board? I'll tell you, it doesn't make you look like a team player."

Victor rubbed his hand over his face but said nothing.

"I mean, I don't know what you think you're accomplishing out there. Do you really think you're going to capture al-Suqqit?"

Victor fought back the urge to scream, "Who the fuck else is going to do it?" The CYA seemed to think it was going to be successful because it had been successful in the past. Wasn't it the CYA's job to catch one of the world's most wanted terrorists? And who better to do that than one of the Agency's counterterrorism officers?

"You know the other thing you can do, just ditch this fucking place and jump on the gravy train of the private contractors. That's where I'm going next. Same fucking job, but twice the salary. And fewer rules. I mean, you'll still be in Rubblestan. We're in a war, and a war means there's lots of money to be made." He paused for a second. "Don't tell anyone I told you that."

Victor had to admire the organization's leaders. They had worked out an ingenious system. Through lack of vision and an overabundance of bureaucracy, they had assured their organization would be incapable of providing policymakers the information and services they needed, thus leading to the hiring of private contractors, who were not constricted by Congressional oversight. But these contractors were all old CYA hands and were ready to hire their old buddies from the organization for a lot of money. Everybody was scratching everybody's back. Except for the soldiers and Marines who actually had to fight in this war. Nobody was scratching their backs and, Victor guessed, they weren't exactly getting rich.

"Think about it, Victor. You've got options. But don't waste your time in the field."

CHAPTER FORTY-SIX
ATLANTA

The store was the biggest Omar had ever seen. He thought it might even be bigger than all of Caliphate Crossing, and it was certainly more open and inviting than the maze of cave tunnels in Rubblestan. He looked for the entrance to the giant blue box and found it under the enormous yellow letters, IKEA.

The rental office and one of Omar's neighbors, who had brought Omar a freshly baked pie—that was quite nice of her, he had thought, before trying to remind himself he was still there to terrorize her—had both commented on his lack of furniture. In fact, Omar had no furniture whatsoever. He realized that, in order to stem the questions and avoid scrutiny, he needed to fit in, and according to Leyla, getting furniture from IKEA was the way to do it.

Dressed in his new jeans from the Gap, which were made with an amazing combination of denim and Lycra, giving them a wonderful stretchy and comfy feel, and a T-shirt that said, "You Don't Know Me... Witness Protection Program," Omar wandered into the first living room he saw in IKEA. He sat on the plush

EKTORP sofa and ran his hand across its BLEKINGE white stain-resistant environmentally friendly fabric while admiring the FRAMSTA TV/storage combination unit against the wall and the VARMLUFT shade lamp hanging from the ceiling. And the ANDRUP flat-woven rug under the HEMNES mahogany coffee table, well, that was just a touch of fun!

He continued like this through the store, bouncing on the VRETA sleek leather armchair, rolling on the FJELLESE bed, sitting at the PRAGEL countertop pretending to drink a Starbucks Frappuccino, which Leyla had introduced him to that morning. Downstairs in the marketplace, he took nearly an hour to choose his flatware, holding each style to get a good feel for it before settling on the FORNUFT design because of its simplicity. He chose a perky fern to help make his living room a little more cheery and picked up some BJORKEFALL candle holders, along with some nice aromatherapy candles. Nothing connoted terror better than a cinnamon pumpkin scented candle.

He returned home laden with bags and packages, excited to start turning his beige apartment into a vibrant, invigorating, and resplendent terror-planning abode.

CHAPTER FORTY-SEVEN
WASHINGTON, DC

His consultations out of the way, Victor was now free to concentrate on catching terrorists. He went to meet Vanessa at an enoteca on U Street. They had developed a comfortable routine when they were working together in Boston, ending their working days by discussing the case over a bottle of wine and then going to Victor's hotel room for a nightcap.

She had already ordered a bottle of Amarone and was sitting at a tall table for two in the bar area, her long legs crossed in a short skirt, the heel of her stiletto hooked on the crossbeam at the bottom of the chair. He kissed her on the cheek and sat down across from her.

"My god, you look good, Vanessa." Her long chestnut hair cascaded down her back, a few tendrils falling around her face and framing her bright green eyes.

"You look the same. When was the last time you got a haircut?"

"I have no idea. At least I don't have a beard. I did for a while. Nothing good came from it."

"Nothing good ever comes from facial hair." She smiled at him over her glass of wine and then took a deep sip. "I think the last time I saw you was when you and that munchkin visited the FBI office in Boston."

Victor put his forehead in his hand and shook his head as he remembered. "I told him to just show his driver's license to get into the building, but the poor fucking kid wanted so desperately to flash his CYA credentials."

Vanessa laughed as she recalled the scene. "Those building guards didn't have a clue what to do with that, yelling to each other across the lobby. 'Hey, Bernard! This guy says he's with CYA!'"

Victor was clutching his stomach, laughing. "It just echoed over and over. 'CYA CYA CYA.' And Bernard yelling back, 'I thought that was in Langley!'"

They both laughed, shaking their heads, and slowly calmed down and caught their breath. Vanessa picked up her glass again.

"Your email was pretty vague. I'm guessing you didn't want too much information floating out there forever in the ether."

"The less written down the better. I've got a weird case. Ever hear of a company named Pistache?"

Vanessa looked surprised and her eyes narrowed with concern and curiosity. She put down her wine glass. "Yes."

He explained to her the information he had gathered on the Crown Prince, the laundering, and the link to a company in Atlanta. Vanessa listened, nodding occasionally, her lips pursed in concentration. When Victor finished, Vanessa uncrossed her legs and leaned in toward him, eager to share what she knew.

"I was investigating Pistache. A year ago, I got a call from our Malaysian counterpart. They had arrested a US citizen on suspicion of terrorism. Michael Lindun. The guy was running an import-export business out of Kuala Lumpur, a company named Ajax. One of its main clients? Pistache."

"What did you find on the company?"

"That's the funny thing. Nothing. I was shut down before I could get anywhere."

"Shut down? By whom?"

"Senator Dick Redd. Or Dick Head, as I prefer to call him."

"Why would he try to stop your investigation? And how?"

"That took a little digging around on my own to figure out. The senator's got himself a super PAC."

"Money as protected free speech."

"The most expensive free speech money can buy. The best part is anyone can give money, including companies owned by foreigners. Including even companies owned by the Crown Prince of Ombudai, who might have an interest in who gets elected."

Victor slumped back in his chair and crossed his arms while he processed what Vanessa had said. "The Crown Prince has been using Pistache to funnel money to Senator Dick Head's super PAC? How did you find all that out?"

"You know I can't give away my sources and methods, Victor." She winked at him. "Senator Dick Head and my Director play golf most weekends. Sometimes they even join the president on the links. I'm guessing Dick Head caught word my team at the FBI was looking into Pistache and he called in a favor. Officially speaking, I'm no longer investigating the company."

"What if I told you I thought the Core was using the company to plot something in Atlanta?"

Vanessa thought about it for a moment. "I've got a friend out there I can call. But I'd stay away from doing anything on the record."

"Heaven forbid we let out Directors know we're actually doing our jobs." They clinked their glasses together and drank down the rest of the wine.

***

Senator Richard Redd had a long history working in politics, even when he had been a businessman. His dad was a former senator and a past Director of CYA and all those contacts were open to Little Dickie as he took over the Redd family peanut business. He did his best, with breakfasts, lunches, and trips to Saint Andrews to make sure the regulatory framework regarding peanut production, import, and export remained friendly. He also made sure that Washington's climate remained beneficial for his friends overseas who shared in his business ventures, and they did the same for him in their capitals. If they all helped each other, he believed, it was good for business, and good business was good for the country, so he was being virtuous.

His cell phone rang as he entered his office in the Hart Senate Office Building. He still got a thrill every time he saw all these young people running around like gerbils doing his bidding. He clicked his phone to answer it.

"Hello. I've got a pizza delivery for Dick Redd," said the voice on the phone. The speaker had a funny accent the senator couldn't quite place.

"I didn't order pizza."

The voice started laughing uncontrollably. "Dick! It's me! I got you with the pizza joke!"

Dick started laughing out loud and nearly dropped his phone. "Faisal, how do you know the pizza joke? I can't believe you got me!" The two were laughing so hard, anyone listening in on the line would have only heard grunting and strange breathing.

Dick closed the door to his office and sat behind his big desk, still clutching the phone to his ear and giggling. A stuffed hawk was mounted on a pedestal on a table behind him, framed by the enormous window. The taxidermist had spread the hawk's wings to their full four-foot wingspan and angled its head down, so it looked like it was diving after a field rat.

"Listen, Dick." The Crown Prince was still trying to catch his breath. "I wanted to let you know about another check."

"Hold on!" Dick got up from his leather chair and climbed into the window barrel, phone in hand. "If we're going to talk shop, I can't be in my office. We wouldn't want the Federal Elections Commission to audit our finances now, would we?" He swung open the giant window and climbed up to the sill. He dangled his legs over the edge and leaned his head out slightly. As he was doing all this, he could hear the Crown Prince on the other end humming the theme from "Jeopardy."

"OK, Faisal. I am officially not in my office. Talk to me."

"I've got another check coming your way. Sorry to tell you, it has a big fat zero on it." He paused for effect. "Several big fat zeros! With a three in front! Ha ha! Did I scare you? Did you think I was sending a check for zero dollars?"

Dick was laughing again, kicking his feet against the side of the Hart Senate Office Building. "Oh, Faisal. You are too much! OK, OK. I have to go now."

"You have to go vote?"

"Oh, no. Something much more important. I've got a lunch with a lobbyist friend. Remember the one we went scuba diving with in Aruba last month?"

"Of course!"

"Thanks for everything, Faisal. I'll keep my eyes open for that check."

CHAPTER FORTY-EIGHT
ATLANTA

Omar leaned back in his new chair from IKEA and shoveled another pile of Kung Pao chicken straight from the take-out box into his mouth with a pair of chopsticks. An empty egg roll bag and a few ripped up soy sauce packets were spread across the coffee table. Omar's new 52-inch flat screen plasma TV was turned on to a soccer match, the spectators' cheers of *"Olé, olé, olé!"* shaking the window as they came out of the surround sound speakers Omar had installed. He read his Facebook news feed. His friend Zulfikar had posted a photo of his son next to a swimming pool wearing what looked like an explosives belt around his waist. His friend had written, "Future martyr? Just kidding! It's a flotation device! ;-)"

Omar took a last bite and threw the Kung Pao chicken box into the delivery bag. He grabbed his keys and went outside and thrilled at the sound of the tweet his new Mini Cooper made when he clicked the key. He recognized it was not the most practical car for hauling bomb parts, but he hadn't been able to resist the red racing stripes and the deep purring sound of the engine. It made running errands a lot less tedious.

He stopped first at the hardware store, where he bought a twenty-pound bag of nails and goo remover. The nails were for the bomb he was making; the goo remover was for the sticky residue the price sticker had left on his new eco-friendly insulated water bottle. He drove down the street and stood in line for nearly an hour to buy a cupcake at a local bakery. He always chastised himself for doing this; the line was always so long. But once the rich buttercream tickled his tongue, he knew he would do it again. He stopped at Williams Sonoma to buy a waffle maker and arrived just in time to watch a demonstration of the store's new line of omelet pans. Omar applauded when the eggs didn't stick and commented to a woman next to him, "I don't know how she did it. I really don't." He tasted a bread and olive oil sample on the way out. Then he went to buy some new and bigger pants.

Back home that evening, shallots sizzled in the twelve-inch sautéing pan and the aroma of freshly pressed parsley and garlic rose from the marble mortar and pestle sitting on the countertop. In the kitchen, Omar wiped his hands on his apron, which said, "Hail to the Chef!" and he used the remote control to turn up the volume on "Top Chef" after first making sure he was TiVo-ing "Dancing with the Stars." As he sprinkled some lemon juice into the pan, he watched Anthony Bourdain slice an onion without shedding a single tear.

He turned off the stovetop, muted the TV, and collapsed on his loveseat. He glanced out his window and could see a neon Coca-Cola sign in the distance. He took a swig from the Coke bottle sitting on his table. It was almost a shame, he thought, surveying the goods that surrounded him. Then he put his feet up on the table and settled in to watch "Homeland."

CHAPTER FORTY-NINE
WASHINGTON, DC

The National Mall was in full bloom and was teeming with springtime tourists looking like they were blossoming out of their pants from too many funnel cakes sold at the snack truck parked at the curb. Vanessa overtook them one by one as she hurried across the Mall toward FBI headquarters. She entered through a side door, swiped her card, and punched in her code. Her heels clicked on the bland, tiled hallway to her office.

She closed the door and took her work cell phone out of her bag. She turned it off, removed the battery, and threw the pieces on her desk. On her personal cell phone, she called one of her officers in the Atlanta office.

"Hey, Ness," Brian greeted her.

"Hey, Brian. How're things?"

"Not the same since you left, but we're getting by. Calling me from your personal phone I see."

"Consider it a social call."

"I can dream," Brian said. "What's up?'

She gave him the background on Pistache, its subsidiary in Atlanta, its links to the Crown Prince, and his connections to Senator Dick Head. When she mentioned the possible connection to Omar al-Suqqit, Brian made a sound as if he were sucking in air just before going down the biggest drop on a roller coaster.

"Fuck, Ness."

"Yeah, fuck. If this Suqqit guy manages to do whatever it is he's planning to do, try explaining that to Congress."

"I'm not sure how I would explain that to the dead people. Congress could wait till after I deal with that part of it."

"How about we don't get to that point? What can you guys do without raising any red flags?"

"I can make some informal inquiries," Brian said. "Poke around a little, see what I find."

"You rock, Brian. Let me know what you find."

***

The sun peeked through a slit in the curtains and the smell of a fresh spring day in Washington wafted in through the window. Vanessa was in bed, the sheet wrapped around her as she stared at the ceiling and enjoyed the soft light and calmness. Her cell phone ringing on the bedside table broke the serenity, but she grabbed it. It was Brian.

"We found your guy and he's been out of control, Ness. Purchases galore from Best Buy to Victoria's Secret to Williams Sonoma. Either he's falling in love with the West or he's a capitalist terrorist."

"Victoria's Secret?"

"We've seen it before. These guys get out of their oppressive surroundings and go ape shit. But there's more."

"Is this an infomercial?"

Brian ignored her sarcasm. "He's made some big purchases at Home Depot. A few things that might give us, um, pause, shall we say?"

"Like what?" Vanessa said, as Victor walked into the bedroom. He was wearing boxers and a T-shirt and carrying two mugs of coffee. He handed one to Vanessa as she motioned for him to sit down.

"Large quantities of cleaning products, fertilizer, nails, and some fuses."

"That's great news," she said.

"Here's the kicker. All the purchases were made with the same credit card. The credit card connects back to the account of Pistache."

"Thanks, Brian. Let me think this through. I'll be in touch."

After she hung up the phone, Vanessa knew she had to be straight with Victor. She had to put this into official channels now, she said. There was indeed a man in Atlanta who matched the name and description of one of the FBI's most wanted terrorists, and he was shopping to a point that would embarrass Ivana Trump, using a credit card linked to the account of a shell company established by the Crown Prince of Ombudai. This wasn't a coincidence. The FBI had to act.

Ness dressed quickly and went to her office to write up the cable with all the information they had on Pistache and Suqqit and to request permission to run surveillance on him.

Victor sat on the bed in Vanessa's apartment and considered his predicament. He was only in Washington for "consultations." Director expected him to return to Pigallo, but he knew that if he went back now, he would lose control of this case. Director would once again dismiss the evidence and, he guessed, he would soon be sent to participate in another FNU LNU disappearance act. Also, technically, as a CYA agent, what he was allowed to do within the United States was limited. As such, Victor concluded, he—a decade-long case officer in the CYA's Counterterrorism Department—would have to go on leave in order to catch this terrorist. If he stayed at his job, Director would prevent him from doing it.

***

Victor went to Director early the next day, with the idea of going in, requesting leave, and getting out. One singular objective to achieve. But he knew it would take all day. Step two would be contacting Zed and explaining, somehow, that he needed to go on leave in order to continue to do his job.

He went to the Human Resources Department and found two young men, both with their noses in textbooks.

"Excuse me," Victor said and they both raised their heads slowly. They looked exhausted. "I need to request a few days of leave." One of the men, dressed in khakis and a blue button-down shirt, which was only halfway tucked in, pushed his chair back. He struggled to stand up, rubbing his neck under his floppy hair before walking over to Victor. Victor felt kind of sorry to make the guy move.

"Sorry I'm slow. Night classes. They're kicking my ass. Now what exactly did you need?"

"I need to request some leave." Victor paused a moment. "Family matters," he said by way of explanation.

"I'd love to help you, dude. But the system's down." He looked at a powered-down computer on a nearby desk then looked back at

Victor and shrugged. "No telling when it will be back up. Hence the night classes," he said, holding up his textbook to show Victor. "I'm getting an IT degree. To fix the system."

"Couldn't you just call in a service request?" Victor asked.

"Phones are down," he said. "Fixing them requires an online service request. Of course, our computers are down." He pointed to the other young man. "He's working on a telecom degree. To fix the phones."

The other guy gave Victor a slight nod and said, "'Sup?"

"Why don't you go to the office that handles all of it and ask for it all to be fixed?"

"We tried," said the first guy. "First, we had to figure out which office we needed to go to. That was, like, a week." He looked to the other guy for confirmation. The other guy nodded. "Then, we spent a few days in those tunnels underground looking for the office, but we got lost in the corridors. We found a supply of rusting electric carts and some discarded documents saying there are no weapons of mass destruction in Iraq. When we went down the next time, we brought a few days' supply of food and sure enough, by that Thursday, we found it. But the guy who runs the office was out. I could smell curry, so I wonder if he wasn't at Director's Indian cooking class that day. Anyway, he had left a sign on the door that said they only take service requests over the computer or phone. So, you know, we'll just fix it ourselves. We're not big Indian food eaters, and really, who's got time for cooking classes when we've got night school to worry about?"

Victor thanked the two night school students and stopped by Starbucks for some caffeine to help him recover from the conversation and consider his options. He went to the parking lot to recover his cell phone from his car and called Zed.

"You're missing all the fun, Victor. Today is a goat-slaying holiday. Smells like blood everywhere, but we anticipate a helluva barbeque tonight. When the fuck are you coming back?"

This would be a delicate task, Victor realized, explaining the situation to Zed over international phone lines that quite possibly could be listened in on. It would be bad if a West African intelligence service caught wind of what Victor was doing, and even worse if Director found out. "I need to go on leave, Zed."

"Why the fuck is that?"

"Family matters."

"Family matters, my ass."

"You remember the woman I told you about? We're coordinating and cooperating really well. I need to stay with her a bit longer, to see where it leads. But it's promising. Very promising. Of course, staying here makes it a bit hard to stay at work."

"Family matters it is then. I trust you not to sit on your ass while you're on leave. You better keep working hard to get that paycheck you won't be earning."

"I've got some travel planned with her. To see about nuptials."

"Got it. Go into the building then; make the request."

"I tried that. The system is down. The phones too. I'm going to need you to deal with the admin side of it."

"I'd say I'm surprised, except that I'm not. Go do your thing with your girlfriend. I'll handle the rest."

CHAPTER FIFTY
JUST OUTSIDE WASHINGTON, DC

The greens at the Congressional Golf Club were freshly trimmed; the smell of cut grass still hung in the air. Little Dickie lined up his wood with his ball and took a swing. The ball landed short of the green and he threw his club down in a tiff and stomped away, leaving it for the caddy to pick up.

"Don't worry, senator. You got seventeen more to make up for it."

"I just wanted to win, that's all," Little Dickie said. "You're up, Director."

Director-FBI took his swing and saw his ball bounce into the trees running along the side of the fairway. "Are we playing mulligans?" They both giggled.

Little Dickie went over to the golf cart, where his clubs were perched on the back. He pressed down on what looked like a golf club head but was actually a whiskey dispenser and poured a drink. Director-FBI removed a flask from his pocket and took a swig. They jumped in the cart, Director-FBI at the wheel. He floored it. Little Dickie nearly fell out and laughed hysterically the whole ride down to the balls.

When they had both finally calmed down, Director-FBI said to Little Dickie, "How're things going with your re-election campaign?"

"Fantastic. The money keeps rolling in!" He did a little dance while singing, "Money money money!" He poured another whiskey. "I got another boat load coming in this week. Literally, a boat load, as in, I think I will buy a boat with it." He held up his drink and said, "To the Crown Prince!"

Director-FBI toasted with Little Dickie but then changed his tone. "I've got a couple agents who are concerned about the Crown Prince."

"What about him? He's a great guy. Did you know he knows the pizza delivery joke?"

Director-FBI almost choked on his drink. "Ha! Did he get you with that one, too?"

"Tell your agents not to worry."

"I don't know. So much emphasis on terrorism these days. But I don't see how the royals fit into it. I keep telling them, how could an Ombudai royal be involved in anything bad like that?"

"Tell them he knows the pizza delivery joke. That will convince them." They both started laughing again.

Little Dickie continued, "Seriously, Director, it won't help my campaign if your guys are digging around the trash of my principal donor. And you know you'll always be welcome on my new boat."

"No worries, senator." He threw his ball back onto the fairway. "You gonna have fishing equipment on that boat?"

CHAPTER FIFTY-ONE
WASHINGTON, DC

Vanessa returned to her apartment from the office and found Victor in the kitchen roasting garlic and stirring a red sauce, a bottle of wine already opened on the countertop. She hesitated to disturb him, wanting to give him a few more minutes of contentedness before sharing with him Director-FBI's response to her request to be able to put surveillance on al-Suqqit.

He set down the spoon, whisked up two glasses of wine, and kissed her before they walked together to the couch and sat down. Vanessa took a long sip.

"The news is that bad?" Victor asked.

"On the contrary," she said. "Director-FBI hailed my efforts to cooperate and coordinate with the CYA. Another example they can wave in front of the IÜD. But we can't actually do anything."

"That makes it an excellent example to wave in front of the IÜD then."

"We can't look into Pistache or al-Suqqit." She took another swig of wine. "But if we come across any FNU LNUs in the Atlanta area, we can run a surveillance team on them."

Victor couldn't say he was surprised. The Crown Prince had good friends all over town, and Senator Dick Head and his daddy were two of his best friends. They in turn could control many of the strings behind the magic curtain, including the strings attached to Director-FBI. Which is why Victor was somewhat astounded when Vanessa said, "Fuck it. Let's put him under full surveillance anyway." He fell in love with her at that moment.

Victor and Vanessa flew to Atlanta the following day. She told her supervisor she was following up on a FNU LNU case. Brian met them at the airport and drove them to the Atlanta field office. He laid out a map and marked several critical sites, including the mall Omar frequented, his apartment, and the nearby peanut refinery plant.

The three of them planned out a surveillance schedule and Vanessa and Victor familiarized themselves with the map.

CHAPTER FIFTY-TWO
CALIPHATE CROSSING, RUBBLESTAN

Zawiki walked into the conference cave at Caliphate Crossing. He had a poppy seed muffin in one hand and was brushing crumbs out of his beard with the other. He smiled to see the headquarters-based principals involved in the Atlanta operation sitting on a large carpet that had been hand-woven by his six-year-old nephew, whose exquisite work had gotten him named Rubblestan's youngest "Mr. Nimble Fingers." Zawiki sat his plump rear end on the carpet, crossed his legs, and picked at his toenails as he scanned the Caliphate Crossing-based fighters.

With demonstrated gravitas, he said to the young people gathered in front of him, "You are the backbone of this operation." His eyes moved around the circle, looking at each fighter, before he smiled and continued, "As thanks, I am unveiling a new poster we've put together to represent how crucial our headquarters warriors are." He unfurled a poster that showed three jihadists in various militant poses, but all sitting at a computer. The first was wearing a potato sack with cut out eyes over his head while he worked at his computer station. The second wielded a machete in one hand while typing with the other. The third was wrapping a blindfold around his computer's web cam.

Zawiki reached into his satchel. "Here, I've got one for each of you." He pulled out three blankets. "These are new in the gift shop. Very versatile. Look, it can be used as a shawl to keep you warm." Zawiki demonstrated this by wrapping the blanket around his shoulders. "Or as a head covering, for your sister, for example." He placed it over his head. "Or as a prayer rug." He threw the blanket on the floor. "Or as a martyr wrap, if you ever choose to go to the field."

CHAPTER FIFTY-THREE
ATLANTA

Victor, Vanessa, and Brian had Omar under full surveillance and had tapped his cell phone. They sat in a car in the alley behind Omar's apartment and Vanessa researched the cell phone's contact numbers on her laptop.

"Holy shit, he's coming back here," Brian said.

They all shrunk in their seats, but Omar did not look their way. He whistled as he carried a bag of trash to the dumpster. Rather than placing it inside the dumpster, he set it down on the ground and lit the bag on fire.

"He's burning his trash?" Victor asked out loud. "Why the fuck is he burning his trash? Don't the neighbors notice that kind of thing?"

Vanessa continued tapping away on her laptop and let out an incredulous, "What the fuck?" Brian and Victor turned their eyes away from the flaming heap of garbage and toward Vanessa. "Does this guy want to get caught? First he uses a credit card that's easily traced to the Crown Prince and his past shady dealings, and now his phone? The phone he's using was used in Buffalo a few months ago by a member of a sleeper cell that was picked up while getting ready to blow up the city hall. The guy's in jail, but his phone ends up in Suqqit's hands? Pretty shoddy operational work."

"Maybe now the terrorists are using trainees like we do," Victor said. Vanessa and Brian gave him a doubtful look. "Seriously. My trainee desk officer has whole departments chasing after people with no names. It's not so far-fetched a new terrorist wouldn't know the one phone, one operation rule. Suqqit probably doesn't even know he's using a dirty phone."

They looked back at Omar, who had returned to his apartment and was sitting on his open windowsill whistling.

"So this guy is a victim of his own bureaucracy?" Brian asked.

"It almost makes me feel bad for him," Victor said.

***

Sitting in his windowsill watching his trash burn below, Omar pulled up Twitter on his new laptop to check out the Core in the Desert's propaganda campaign. The last two tweets from his group read, "Death to America!" and "Down with the West!" Even he wasn't inspired; the tweets lacked creativity. He made a mental note to hire someone to improve their outreach once he returned to the DRZ.

Inside, the very large head of Glenn Beck was squawking from Omar's big screen TV. He was bashing a proposal to raise taxes, saying it was a form of "fiscal terrorism." Last week, someone else had described Beck and his political compatriots as "terrorists" because they were supposedly holding the country's debt hostage for political reasons. Omar resented how the Americans threw this term around. He and his colleagues worked hard to earn this moniker, painstakingly plotting to bring down all of Western civilization. They went through hours of rigorous training and indoctrination, and they had to learn the intricacies of running an operation and making something go boom. Omar felt insulted.

He decided to go out for a walk to calm his nerves before tomorrow's big event. He turned off Glenn Beck and walked out onto the warm Atlanta streets. He wandered into a park, where a young man had set up a stall selling peanuts. The line to buy them was long. Large, happy Americans would wait for hours to be able to consume this salty treat.

Omar sat on a bench and watched them. With each purchase, he felt himself get angrier. This mass consumption, he thought bitterly, it was to blame. The money from this peanut consumption flowed back in waves to West Africa and helped keep the dictators in power and the people oppressed. Profits from this consumption went into the leaders' private coffers. The West African people were not benefiting from this. They didn't see a hospital get built with the profits, or a school for their children. The United States was to blame for this.

Feeling empowered and fortified for the next day, Omar stopped at Leyla's. They had planned to pick up the truck together that evening, plus Omar wanted to see how she was doing as the event approached. After all, she would be the one driving the truck. Omar was only going to help load it; the skills of emirs were to be preserved for future attacks.

Leyla was at the salon next door to her apartment getting waxed. "You didn't want to shave?" he asked her.

"Trust me, this is more of a sacrifice," she said. She winced in pain as all her body hair was ripped off. Omar sat in a bright purple chair in the window and waited for her to complete her ritual. She was positively glowing when she was done.

They took a taxi together to the truck rental office. Omar marked the taxi receipt for accounting purposes. The teenage kid working behind the truck rental desk led them out to the last remaining truck on the lot. He held up the keys, not sure to whom to give them. Leyla glanced at Omar with a smile and then gently took the keys out of the teenager's hands. She climbed into the cab of the truck as Omar climbed in on the passenger side.

Leyla placed the key in the ignition, using only her index finger and thumb and keeping the other fingers and their fresh polish safe from being chipped, and turned it. The truck lurched but the engine did not turn over.

"Gotta put the clutch in," the teenager said, picking at a pimple.

"Clutch?" Leyla asked.

Omar turned to her, holding his breath, working up the courage to ask a question he was afraid to hear the answer to. "You do know how to drive a manual transmission, don't you, Leyla?"

She looked befuddled. "Manual what?"

Omar said a silent prayer. "Do you have any automatic transmissions?" he asked the teenager.

"All sold out, mister. Big antique convention this weekend. There's nothing at any of our branches."

Omar got out of the truck and circled around to Leyla's side and he motioned for her to slide over. She did and he took the wheel. He thanked the teenager and pulled out of the parking lot. He tried to stay calm, but he couldn't help feeling a little nervous, with all the last minute details that needed his attention. The bomb still needed to be assembled in the back of the truck. He had wanted to pick up another bag of nails for the shrapnel, just in case. Plus, he had really been hoping to have time to pick up a rotisserie chicken for dinner. He had been craving one since lunchtime. He also had laundry to do and dirty dishes were piling up in the kitchen. He still had not worked out where his dishwasher was and why she had not reported to his apartment. And now, he realized, he had to teach Leyla how to drive a stick shift. She was due to drive it to the target in just over twelve hours.

He drove to a cemetery not far away. It was a good place to teach the martyr video diva how to drive, and the chances were low that someone could get hurt, since the majority of people there were already dead. It was also a good choice because between the cemetery and Omar's apartment was a great rotisserie chicken place, so he could stop by and pick up dinner on his way home.

He gave Leyla back the driver's seat. He pointed out the gearshift and explained that she needed to find a balance between the clutch and the accelerator. Awkwardly, she shifted into first gear. As she let up on the clutch, the truck pitched forward and then stalled. She smiled at Omar and tried again.

***

Victor, Vanessa, and Brian followed Omar and Leyla to the cemetery. When they had seen the two of them go to the truck rental shop, they had each shuddered. They agreed they wanted to arrest them tonight. The truck could only mean one thing. But arresting them was going to be difficult, considering they weren't supposed to be following them in the first place. Technically there was nothing illegal about the purchases they had made, and renting a truck was hardly against the law. They watched the truck jump forward and stall, jump forward and stall, again and again.

"We may not have to stop them," Brian said. "I'm not sure they can even get the truck to the site." The truck's wheels turned in place, making a screeching sound before the engine stalled again.

"The truck bomber who couldn't drive. It's a nice touch," said Victor.

"We have to wait till the bomb is loaded and they're on their way to the site," Vanessa said. "An empty truck with a cute twenty-year-old driver will get us nothing. Except a cable from the IÜD warning field agents that young people drive vehicles and we should coordinate and cooperate with each other to determine the pertinent threat matrix application."

"You said that a little too easily," Victor said to her.

"How do you think I made it to management? Now what the fuck is our plan?"

***

Within a few hours, Leyla was getting a hang of how to handle the clutch, so much so that Omar suggested she drive him home.

Victor, Vanessa, and Brian followed the truck out of the cemetery. It slowly turned a corner, idled a little too long at a stop sign, then pulled in with a screech to a rotisserie chicken shop. They saw Omar and Leyla jump out of the truck.

"Can I run in and get some mashed potatoes?" Brian asked. Vanessa and Victor both smirked and dismissed him. "What? I'm just asking. I'm hungry. And the gravy here is really good."

Omar and Leyla came out of the chicken place with bags of food. Omar was holding a drumstick and wore a huge smile and Leyla nibbled at a piece of lettuce as they piled back into the truck, which Victor, Vanessa, and Brian followed back to Omar's apartment.

Leyla jumped out from the driver's side, while Omar stepped to the curb, juggling bags of food. She circled around and kissed Omar on the cheek as she said a quick goodnight. Before she turned to walk home, she asked, "Breakfast at IHOP before we head to the refinery?"

"Someone wants blueberry pancakes before she self-detonates!"

Leyla smiled and looked down. "I'll come by early?"

"Yes, my dear. We'll load the truck then go for pancakes. Go get some rest now."

She turned to walk away. Omar followed her with his gaze until she waved and disappeared around the corner.

***

The following morning, the sun was shining brightly and so was Leyla as she nearly skipped to Omar's apartment. Omar was putting the final touches on the bomb parts to be loaded into the truck. The two went into his kitchen to get some tea and Omar watched as Leyla opened the metal contraption next to the sink and placed her dirty mug inside one of the sliding plastic drawers.

"What are you doing?" he asked.

"Putting my dirty cup in the dishwasher. You should probably do the same with all these dishes," she said. Leyla pointed to the pile of dishes with food crusted on them, hoping not to embarrass him.

"*This* is a dishwasher in America?"

"Yes, Omar. What did you think it was?"

Omar leaned back against the counter. His hand went to his head, which he shook in disbelief for several seconds. "All this time

I was waiting for her. And here she is. Only she is a machine. This seems very American to me."

Leyla went back out to the living room and sat on Omar's chair. Faruk had arrived and began outfitting her with a camera on her head. Omar returned to the bomb and tried to concentrate but kept getting distracted by Faruk admonishing Leyla to sit still. He preferred wiring a bomb in peace.

"This has never been done before," Faruk said, his hands spread wide and tapping the air for emphasis. "This will be the ultimate in ultimate sacrifice." He stood back to admire his handiwork before clapping his hands to get Omar's attention. "I present to you, the Martyr Cam!" He paused to allow Omar to be in awe for a moment. "This will capture the operation from your point of view, Leyla. The Core is now filming all its operations for training and recruitment purposes. A recent video got nine million hits on YouTube."

"Won't the camera blow up with me?" Leyla asked.

"Yes, it will. But the recording is controlled remotely and the footage is instantly downloaded onto my computer."

"Couldn't we control the truck remotely, too, then?" Leyla asked.

"That would defeat the purpose of a martyrdom operation, my dear."

"I see your point," she conceded.

Omar focused on the bomb in front of him, reading the instructions provided by the bomb maker three times to be sure he was connecting the wires correctly. The instructions were quite good, he thought. Easier to follow than the IKEA drawings for his furniture. Faruk was checking the sound levels as Leyla practiced yelling, "Allahu Akbar!" over and over again.

Omar gave the bomb a last look and then turned to Faruk and Leyla. It was time.

Victor, Vanessa, and Brian sat up in their seats when they saw Omar and Leyla coming out of the building.

"What is that on her head?" Victor asked, motioning toward Leyla. She wore what looked like a thick headband across her forehead and she looked like she was concentrating very hard on keeping her head still. A short man wearing a red fez followed her. He kept saying, "Keep your chin up, dear. Chin up. No one wants to see the sidewalk." Omar had a large black case in his hands.

"Could someone open the back of the truck for me, please?" Omar asked, but Faruk and Leyla continued fussing with the camera. Omar tried to balance the case in one hand while he fished in his pocket for the truck keys. He nearly dropped the case, recovering the balance just before it fell. He barely managed to open the back of the truck and set the case down. He wiped his brow as he heard Faruk say to Leyla, "Make me a believer."

When everything was loaded, Leyla climbed into the driver's seat with Omar next to her and Faruk shoved in the back. The truck took off with Victor, Vanessa, and Brian following.

As soon as they pulled onto the highway, Omar deeply regretted he had chosen this route. Traffic was at a near standstill. He had wanted to test the route at several different times of day, but Core Central had dismissed this request as part of its "Going Green" initiative. They sat in traffic as Omar studied the map and saw that the first exit was at least two miles ahead, and that alternate route didn't allow for them to stop at IHOP, as he had promised Leyla.

They sat in silence in the traffic. Leyla smiled at Omar, her eyes cast down slightly. He smiled back. She clicked on the radio. Eddie

Money's "Two Tickets to Paradise" was playing on the classic rock station. The traffic didn't move.

Omar looked at his watch, then at the traffic, then back at Leyla. "We might have to skip IHOP, my dear, and go straight to the target."

Leyla nodded. She looked sad.

"You'll have pancakes tonight in Paradise, topped with berries and passion fruit."

"I understand," she said in a quiet voice without looking at him. "They're just.... IHOP makes really good pancakes, that's all. And I didn't eat breakfast. I thought we were going for pancakes. I hope I don't faint from lack of food."

Omar had to admit that would be bad and he recognized the need to keep Leyla happy. Zawiki would block any future operations by Omar if his martyr passed out before she could detonate the bomb. "There's a Denny's just outside the refinery's gates. Will that do, dear?"

Leyla let out a triumphant, "Yes!" and immediately turned up the volume on the radio. She sang out loud with the song, tailoring the words for her own situation. "I've got one ticket to Paradise!"

**

"They must be heading to the refinery," Brian said when at last the truck pulled off at an exit after a seemingly interminable period sitting in traffic. "Wait, they're pulling in to the Denny's."

"Who the fuck eats at Denny's before bombing themselves to heaven?" Vanessa asked.

"I don't know. I might order the Rooty Tooty Fresh 'N Fruity if it were my last meal," Brian said.

"I thought that was IHOP," Vanessa said to him.

"I thought IHOP was the Grand Slam."

Victor interrupted them. "Maybe this culinary debate could wait till after we catch the terrorists and save the world from total annihilation?"

Vanessa and Brian looked at Victor. He couldn't tell if they were sheepish or annoyed, but Vanessa established control again. "Follow them in."

Leyla parked the truck in the Denny's parking lot and stepped out of the vehicle, balancing the camera on her head and trying to remember to keep her chin up, as Faruk had instructed. "Don't eat too much, dear!" he called out to her. "Those virgins have many venerated to choose from, you know."

Vanessa, Victor, and Brian pulled into the lot.

"All right, guys. We pick them up," Vanessa said, adjusting the gun in her holster and pulling her jacket down over it. She turned to Victor and hesitated. "You have to stay in the car."

"Are you crazy?" he asked.

"If they catch you near this, working on American soil, Congress will have a fucking field day writing up new regulations."

"I can see it now," Brian said, taking Vanessa's side. "Regulation FU 6014: The CYA shall not engage in terrorist investigations in the homeland but shall be held responsible when those terrorists go ballistic. Then they'll ship your headquarters to Canada or something."

"That might not be a bad idea," Victor said. "Moving Director far, far away from Washington. But you're seriously going to make me sit this out?"

"If you come along, it could screw up the entire judicial proceeding. Working in the US, we have to consider the fourth amendment, how evidence is collected, and all kinds of other legal regulations you've never had to think about in your line of work. Stay here. Let us do this."

Victor was angry. He knew she was right, but he had been chasing Omar al-Suqqit across the globe, fighting against Joseph the Support Officer for a comfortable chair that was above his pay grade, nearly shooting an officer in Rubblestan who was blindly celebrating the ambassador's well-intentioned but wholly inconsiderate *Shalwar Kameez* Day, beating away a rabid dog with a bobble-head Jesus. He couldn't help but want to bring Omar al-Suqqit down himself. But he forced himself to stay in the car, while Vanessa and Brian went into the restaurant.

The two FBI agents looked from table to table. The Tuesday morning crowd consisted mostly of retirees, some of whom were animatedly debating the benefits and risks of Viagra. "I don't see why four hours is bad," one woman was saying. "I wish it *would* last four hours." Vanessa motioned to Brian that they should check the back room.

There, they saw Leyla and the man in the red fez sitting at a round table. From this distance, Vanessa could see that the contraption on the young female terrorist's head was indeed a camera, which was blinking red, indicating the camera was recording the spread of large golden pancakes, fruit salad, and an assortment of eggs. But as Vanessa and Brian scanned the table, they saw one person was missing.

***

Omar ran his hands through the air dryer in the bathroom, amazed with how loud it was, as if he were holding his wet hands up to a jet engine. He loved how the strong air current shook his skin, like the flesh waves on Tom Cruise's face in that "Mission: Impossible" movie. Omar ran his hands through the dryer several more times, even though his hands were already dry. He exited the bathroom and went back out to the dining area, rubbing his warm hands together in anticipation of a good, solid American breakfast. As he turned the corner toward the table, he saw a man and a woman brandishing what looked like shiny badges. The woman had Leyla bent over the table and was handcuffing her. Leyla kept trying to keep her chin up and Omar could see that her camera was still filming. Omar then saw the man slap handcuffs on Faruk, whose red fez fell off into a plate of strawberry jam.

Omar froze in place, he didn't know for how long. Suddenly, his wits returned and he knew what he needed to do.

***

Victor was restless in the back of Brian's car. He kept muttering the word "fuck" to no one in particular. Sometimes he would scream it while slamming a fist into the car door. *Fuck it, I'm going in.* He opened the door and had one foot on the ground when he saw Omar walk out the front door of Denny's, alone. Victor didn't move as he watched Omar get into the truck and begin backing out.

"What the fuck?" Victor practically screamed. He jumped out of Brian's car and ran up from behind the truck to the passenger door. As Omar was driving out of the parking lot, Victor managed to grab the door handle, open it, and jump in. Omar was shocked and started yelling, "Who are you? Get out!" In his panic, he could not stop the truck and bumped out into traffic before regaining control.

"Keep driving," Victor said, still not sure what his next move was going to be.

Rattled, Omar looked at Victor, then back at the road, then at Victor again. They sat in silence for a moment as the truck weaved through traffic before Omar said, "I know who you are."

Victor said nothing.

"I knew it." Omar shook his head in frustration. He slammed the steering wheel with his hand. "I knew it! I knew that tubby weasel would send someone to check up on me. Didn't think I could handle the Big Time. Oh, he's going to love this. Have you told him already? Go ahead, send the cable. Tell that muffin-eating fat ferret that al-Suqqit screwed up. Tell him it was my fault. Not that I didn't try. Oh, I tried! But how can I keep Leyla inconspicuous when she has a camera strapped to her head? That idea came from Core Central. For all I know, Zawiki turned us in to the FBI, just to spite me. Then he sends you to check up on me. How long have you been following me? When did Zawiki send you?"

"Zawiki didn't send me," Victor said.

"Then who are you?"

"I work for the CYA," Victor said, exasperated. "I'm here to capture you, not check up on you!"

Omar furrowed his brow in confusion and looked again at Victor. "The CYA? How did you find me?"

"I'm not going to tell you that," Victor said in a high-pitched voice.

Omar stopped the truck at a red light. He turned to face Victor directly. "Are you arresting me?"

Victor hesitated. How could he arrest Omar? He wasn't law enforcement. Technically he wasn't even CYA at this moment, since he had taken leave in order to stay in Atlanta and help Vanessa and Brian capture the terrorist he now found himself sitting next to in a rented truck with a giant bomb in the back. He took his cell phone out of his pocket to call Vanessa. As he pulled up her number, both Victor and Omar heard the wailing sirens of a police car behind them. A scratchy voice said through a speaker, "Pull over." Omar and Victor looked at each other and Victor flipped his phone shut. Victor smiled. "Those are my friends." Omar nervously maneuvered the truck through the traffic and to the side of the road.

A member of Atlanta's finest approached the driver-side window and knocked on it. Omar fiddled with all the different buttons on his door, trying to roll down the window. He pushed one and felt his seat slowly sinking. He tried another and saw the side-view mirror move. Finally, he managed to find the right one and he rolled down the window while smiling at the officer. "Good day, sir."

"I'm afraid it's not a good day," the officer said from behind reflective sunglasses. "Any day when I see people who can't follow the most basic of rules, the most preventive of measures, is not a good day in my book. You gentlemen are not wearing seatbelts. It's the simplest thing to do, but you're not doing it. I'm going to have to cite you for it."

Victor leaned forward and said, "Officer, arrest this man. He's on the FBI's Most Wanted List and he has a bomb in the back of the truck."

"Aren't you clever," the officer said to Victor. "Don't you know it's illegal to falsely report a crime, especially to get out of another crime you are being cited for?"

"I'm not falsely reporting a crime. He's a terrorist," Victor said pointing to Omar. "Tell him you're a terrorist," he said to Omar.

Omar looked back at the officer and smiled. "I don't know this gentleman. He jumped in my car while I was pulling out of a parking lot and he refuses to get out."

"Are you trying to carjack him?" the officer said to Victor. He leaned into the walkie-talkie that was attached to his shoulder. "Jack, we've got a possible carjacking in progress here. Call in for backup."

"No, officer. You have it all wrong," Victor said. "I'm with the CYA. This guy is a terrorist and I've been chasing him all over the world trying to capture him. He was about to deliver this bomb to the peanut refinery up the street in order to blow it up."

"CYA?" the officer snapped at Victor. "CYA isn't allowed to work in this country. Show me some credentials."

"I don't have credentials."

"If you work for the government, you must have a badge. Everyone working for the government has a badge. I've been to Washington. I've seen it. Seems like you can't even get in to happy hour in that city without a badge hanging around your neck."

"Not all CYA officers carry badges that say CYA. I work undercover."

"This is getting better every minute. You work undercover so of course you don't have a badge. That's convenient."

"Here's my license. Call the FBI's Atlanta office, you'll see I'm here working with them."

The officer took Victor's license and returned to his car. Omar and Victor sat in silence, staring straight ahead. After a minute, Omar started whistling "Once Upon a Time in the West." Victor gave him a dirty look. The officer came back.

"You two need to step out of the car. Looks like we do indeed have a terrorist situation on our hands."

"Thank you!" Victor said to the officer and opened his door. Before he could step all the way out, he was handcuffed by another officer. "What the fuck are you doing?"

"Easy, Mr. Qu'aro. Nice work changing the Arabic spelling of your name on your license. C-A-R-O, my ass. Don't worry. We'll be bringing down your document forger, too. We'll get that information from you during your interrogation."

"Are you fucking kidding me?" Victor yelled. He looked across the hood of the truck. Omar was listening to the first officer.

"I'm afraid you're going to have to come down to the station with us so we can get a full statement from you on this terrorist who tried to carjack you. I still have to cite you for not wearing your seatbelt."

"I understand," Omar said.

"We've got a tow truck on the way to take your vehicle to the station."

Omar nodded and followed along as the officer led him to the police car. The second officer was shoving Victor into the back seat. "Call the fucking FBI!" he was yelling. "You fucking idiots! I'm not the fucking terrorist here!"

The first officer said to Omar, "My partner's got to ride up here with me, but don't worry. He's cuffed," he said, pointing to Victor, who was kicking the back of the police car's front seat and banging his head against the plastic grill partition between the front and back seats. "He can't hurt you anymore." The policeman opened the back door of the police car for Omar. He slid in silently next to Victor, who was now slumped forward with his forehead resting against the partition grill. He looked completely dejected.

The police car took off in the direction of the police station just as the tow truck arrived and the driver began hooking it up to

Omar's rental truck. The police car pulled into the same morning traffic Victor felt like he had been sitting in for hours. After a few minutes, he turned to the man he had been chasing across the globe.

"Do you have any idea what I've been through trying to catch you?"

Omar looked at Victor. Victor's hair was a mess, as if he had just been through a windstorm, and his forehead was covered with red crisscross marks from the grill of the partition. Omar could see a distinct wariness behind his eyes, which seemed almost to plead with Omar to help him, to quit the terrorist fight. Omar felt an incredible urge to give in to the impulse and do just that.

"I had to fill out a ten-page travel authorization form, justifying my reasons for bringing more than a carry-on bag to Rubblestan, since checking luggage was an added fee, and explaining why the trip was necessary. I am a counterterrorism officer at the CYA and I have to justify my traveling to a war zone where the terrorists are fighting our troops. Worse, I had to redo the form because I originally filled it out in blue ink, not black, which is the preferred ink color of the support officer who insists that I sit on a rusty, broken chair that perfectly symbolizes where I sit on the middle management ladder. I had to fill out another form—this one was eleven pages—for the Intelligence Über Director, who wanted exactly the same information but in a different order. And then, before my tickets could be issued, I was told to fill out EATME, the Employee Airline Travel Management Entity, which asked for *all the same fucking information*. Then, when I was leaving, the support officer actually asked me, I shit you not, where I was going. And like I really wanted to go to Rubblestan in the first place! That country is literally just piles of rubble. Rubble everywhere. I've never seen so many useless pieces of rubble just piled everywhere. And nothing else. Only rubble. And terrorists. Rubble and terrorists. That's it. Yet I spent an entire fucking day filling out forms to get to that paradise of pebbles."

Victor turned to look out the window. His wrists hurt. He shifted his weight to try to stop the handcuffs from rubbing so much. He stared at the traffic outside. It was quiet in the car for a moment. Then Victor heard Omar whisper as he gazed out his own window.

"They removed our Reply All function."

Victor turned toward Omar and said with annoyance, "What?"

"They removed our Reply All function. One day, Core Central Leadership sent an email to all the Core franchises asking for suggestions for improving the vegan selection of food in the cafeteria. Core Central intended, of course, for people to send their suggestions back, but one warrior hit Reply All, letting us all know where he stood on tofu in a bean and wasabi sauce. Then others wanted to spread their ideas, too. And everyone started to Reply All. Hundreds of emails were going to thousands of fighters around the world. The system crashed. Core Central's solution was to remove Reply All. They kept serving the tofu."

"That's not such a bad idea actually," Victor said.

"Tofu? It's very healthy."

"No, removing the Reply All."

"Right, unless you are the media official for your franchise and your job is to keep hundreds of journalists aware of your activities. My press guy, for example. Each time the Core in the Desert is mentioned in an article, he sends out a copy to every media outlet, to let them know we're still relevant. Now, to send out a group email, he has to type in each email address individually. Do you know how long that takes him? That's valuable time that he could be spending writing up a news release about how the Great Enemy is trying to indoctrinate our children with a brainwashing drug distributed through Coca-Cola."

Victor was looking at Omar with astonished eyes. He turned his body so he was facing him directly.

"Do you know the psych assessment I had to go through to get this job? How many times I've been asked if I hear voices or if I try to interpret my morning shits like they're Turkish coffee stains?"

"To make the Brotherhood a Core franchise, I had to write two essays, including one describing martyrdom. In five hundred words or less. They sent it back to me because I was over by three words. I didn't know they would count the date as three words!"

"A few weeks ago, I spent an entire day strapped to a machine and telling the raw truth of my life to a lemon-sucking rodent in chinos, and then spent the entire night lying to my closest friends about what I've been doing all these years. Of course, the truth is that I spend most of my time filling out forms. I've become my own secretary." Victor leaned in toward Omar. Omar leaned in, too. "You remember a couple of years ago, when you guys blew up that toothpaste factory in Pigallo just after our president visited?"

"I remember that. We thought it was a good symbol of the Great Enemy, since you all have such nice teeth. I admit, we hadn't thought that one all the way through. We should have realized all the workers were Pigallese. We ended up killing our own. Core Central made us implement a new Lethal Liability metric because of that," Omar said as he rolled his eyes.

"I'm watching the destruction on TV in the office. Flames and blood everywhere. And my boss at the time walks up to me and hands me a survey about how I feel working on counterterrorism operations and whether I feel effective in my job, and he asks that I please turn it in that same day."

Victor and Omar were now huddled together like two teenage girls discussing what some slut did for seven minutes in Joey's closet last weekend.

"Did you see that camera we put on Leyla's head?" Omar asked. "Core Central laid out specific standards for how we could attach it to her. We had to buy specially manufactured, non-pinching elastic straps. The girl is about to blow her entire body apart, and Core Central wants to make sure the camera strap doesn't pinch her skin."

"I've dedicated my entire professional life to stopping terrorists, and I got put on the Terrorist Watch List."

"Ouch," Omar said.

Victor slumped back in his seat, looking tired. He dropped his head back on the headrest, which was too low, and spoke quietly while staring at the ceiling. "And now I've been arrested for being a terrorist, while I was trying to stop a terrorist driving a bomb-laden truck."

Omar turned back toward his window and nodded. The police car pulled in to the station.

One of the officers opened Victor's door, grabbed his arm, and pulled him inside the building. The other officer offered a hand to help Omar out of the back seat. He jogged past Omar, opened the building's front door, and bowed slightly as he gestured for Omar to go in. Victor was placed in a holding cell and told to turn around and place his hands near the bars, so the officer could remove his handcuffs. Omar was told to take a seat next to a desk, just outside the cell. Victor dropped onto a bench and rubbed his hands over his face while letting out a cry of frustration.

"I'm really sorry. This was never against you," Omar said.

"I'm afraid I can't return the sentiment. For me, this was always about you. But it turned into being about the bureaucracy."

They sat in silence for a few minutes.

The sound of a commotion outside broke their reverie. From his cell, Victor had to tweak his neck to get even a miniscule view out the front door. Omar got up to look. He froze when he saw the bomb squad descend on his rented truck, which had been parked in the police station's lot. He turned in a panic, trying to find another door through which he could escape, but Vanessa came barreling through the door where he was standing and handcuffed him without a word. An Atlanta police officer followed her in and they both took Omar by an elbow and threw him into the same holding cell with Victor.

"Ness?" Victor said. "What happened?"

"Sorry it took us a while to get here. We came out of Denny's and saw the truck and you were gone. We figured you had followed Suqqit." She glanced at Omar, who was settling onto the bench where Victor had been sitting. "Looks like we were right. On our way to bring in the others, we saw the truck being towed. Since the FBI can only interact with the local police through the Atlanta fusion center, it took some time for everyone to agree on who had the authority to call the bomb squad."

"At least you managed finally to cut through that red tape."

"Not really. I sent Brian there to work it out. Then I called my friend Hank who's on the squad and told him what was happening.

They should have official authorization by tomorrow to dismantle the bomb, but Hank decided to go ahead and do it now, rather than waiting for the proper paperwork to go through. He'll forward date the forms to tomorrow. That bomb would have taken out half a mile around."

"Can I get out of here now please?" Victor asked.

Vanessa gave Victor an apologetic look. "I'm afraid that part isn't quite as easy."

"What?"

"They think you were an accomplice since you were in the truck and your name is on the Terrorist Watch List." Victor began to protest but Vanessa cut him off. "I've already called a friend at the Department of Homeland Security, but, you know, my request has to work its way through the system."

Victor looked at Omar, who was biting his nails. He turned back toward Vanessa and hit his forehead against the prison bars.

"I'm going to get you out," Vanessa assured him. "I just need a little time." Her phone rang and she stepped away from the jail cell to answer it. Victor sat down next to Omar, who turned to him and smiled, despondent.

After a few minutes, Vanessa returned. "You've got a one-way ticket to Cuba, Mr. al-Suqqit, on your very own privately chartered plane. You leave in three hours."

Omar did not say anything. He leaned back against the cold cell wall and nodded.

"Victor..." she began.

He shook his head. "I know. You have to go. There must be quite a few forms you have to fill out to charter a plane to Cuba."

"I'll deal with that after. Easier to ask for forgiveness than permission, right? Anyway, between the FBI, the local police, you guys, and the military running the detention facility, not to mention Justice having to write at least three reports, it will take a few days to even figure out which forms I need to fill out. But I'm not abandoning you. I'm going to get you out. I promise."

"Go already," he said. She walked out of the police station and Victor found himself once again pounding his head against the wall.

CHAPTER FIFTY-FOUR
WASHINGTON, DC

Senator Dick Redd was pretending a sugar packet was a race car driving at furious speeds through a city made up of salt and pepper shakers and a pitcher of fresh-squeezed orange juice. He made the sounds of screeching tires

"I hope you're pretending it's a Ferrari, senator," said a voice behind him.

Little Dickie turned around and his face lit up to see his good friend. "Faisal!" he said, hugging the Crown Prince. "I'm so glad you could make it!"

"You know I never pass up breakfast at the Ritz Carlton. I just love the little umbrellas they put in the drinks. So festive, don't you think?"

"Thank you again, Faisal, for your last contribution," Little Dickie said as the Crown Prince took a seat. "With that donation we were able to run an attack ad against my opponent claiming he went to college and reads books."

"That's harsh."

"That kind of behavior doesn't sit well with my constituents. Next ad, we're going to highlight how he tries to help the poor."

"That poor soul," said the Crown Prince. "No pun intended!" They both broke out in a fit of laughter.

Another voice came from behind them. "This doesn't look like a serious breakfast meeting." The Crown Prince and Little Dickie stopped laughing and looked at each other with wide eyes before turning around to see Director-FBI standing over their table. They erupted in laughter again and the Director joined in.

"Sit! Sit, Director," the Crown Prince managed to say in between chortles.

It took a few minutes before they were calm enough to look at each other without breaking into roars of laughter. As the waitress served them their lox and bagels, Little Dickie got down to business.

"I understand you have an investment proposal for us, Faisal?"

"Indeed I do, senator. One of my companies has been surveying for new peanut fields in the Democratic Republic of Zuzu. We think we've found some potential ground, but deep down. It will require a bit more geological exploration and some drilling."

"Deep ground peanut harvesting. It sounds interesting," said Little Dickie. Director-FBI nodded in agreement.

The Crown Prince continued, "The return could be huge, of course, as long as..."

Director-FBI's phone rang, interrupting the Crown Prince.

"This better be important, Carol. I'm in the middle of an important breakfast." Director-FBI looked at the Crown Prince as he spoke, to assure him that he was still the Director's priority. "I thought I told them *not* to do that?" He paused. "Really? Like the kind that goes boom?" He listened to Carol. "But not a big bomb, right? Half a mile? Is that big, as bombs go?" He thought for a moment. "Carol, listen. I'm in a very important meeting." He winked at the Crown Prince. "Let me finish up, then I'll come in."

He put his phone down on the table and apologized to the Crown Prince. "That was my office. Some of my field agents just picked up an Omar al-Suqqit with a bomb in the back of his truck. He was heading toward a peanut refinery in Atlanta."

"That will be great for my campaign," the senator said. "I can say we stopped a terrorist! A terrorist who wanted to do evil because of my opponent!"

"Georgia isn't your state, is it, senator?" the Crown Prince asked.

"No, but we'll find a way to spin this in my favor. We always do."

"That's great, Dickie! Then I'll be able to get you even more money!" The Crown Prince and Senator Dickie grinned like schoolboys who had snuck into the girls' locker room after gym class.

Director-FBI continued, "He's been using a credit card linked to one of your companies, Faisal." He turned to the senator. "The same company that was giving money to your super PAC, Dick."

Little Dickie, the Crown Prince, and Director-FBI looked at each other without a word. Each man was contemplating his next move. If they each played this correctly, it could mean endless political and monetary gain for all three. But if the delicate balance between them was upset in any way, it could mean the end to each one's power. They all recognized the benefits of working through this together. Director-FBI spoke first.

"We need to get you out of the country, Crown Prince. You and any relatives you have here in the United States. I know you aren't personally involved. I understand these nuances, but not all Americans do. They could seek retribution. I can arrange to have a plane pick up you and your family members, wherever they are, and fly you all out tonight before anyone can ask too many questions."

They all nodded in agreement.

"I guess I need to prepare a statement for the press," Senator Dick Head said.

They nodded at that, as well.

They stood up and shook hands, and each went his separate way.

***

John Boy sat at his desk with a cup of coffee in hand and decided to scroll through cables on monitor number three to try to find inspiration for what color should represent "Victory!" on his new threat level color chart. He searched the word "Victory" and saw the subject line, "Request to remove CYA officer Victor Caro from the Terrorist Watch List and release him from prison." John Boy opened the cable and was shocked the Victor he knew was considered a terrorist. He pulled up some background information then decided to go see his advisor.

John Boy entered his supervisor's office, closed the door behind him, and flipped a switch. The glass wall of the office immediately smoked up, giving them privacy and signaling to John Boy's supervisor, and everyone outside the office, that this was serious.

John Boy explained the situation and laid out his evidence on his supervisor's desk. His supervisor looked over the various cables and correspondence with growing incredulity. "How could this have happened?" he said in total disbelief. "How is this even possible?" He looked across the desk at John Boy. "This is completely wrong."

"Tell me about it," John Boy agreed.

"From start to finish, the whole thing is problematic." The supervisor sat back in his chair and crossed his legs. "First, the officer at the scene who pulled him over never filed form DHS-35X-1, which is so clearly the first thing required under the Patriot Act."

"I know. I couldn't believe it either. Something so obvious," John Boy said.

"Then, the Virginia police never turned in the joint cable with the FBI to the Department of Homeland Security's Office for Terrorist Watch List Protocol Requirements, outlining that all requisite information was included in the proper format."

"Incredible."

"Then," the supervisor said, leaning over his desk and shuffling through the papers there, "the CYA cable requesting a spelling change in the name does not include the proper routing labels, either at the top or at the bottom. Totally unformatted. And where is the original of the Terrorist Watch List template cable? That should have been the first thing written. None of these other cables were supposed to be disseminated without it. Victor's information should have also been entered, separately, into the Terrorist Watch List information database, as well as the Immigration and Customs Enforcement database for suspected terrorists. Plus, the airlines just put this guy on their no-fly list, based on the incomplete information from us. And I say incomplete because, again, that original template cable was never written."

The supervisor sat back again and thought for a full minute. He took a deep breath in and exhaled slowly as he looked at John Boy and shrugged his shoulders. "We can't hold this guy. Without the proper paperwork, he shouldn't be on the Terrorist Watch List at all. Just take him off."

"That's it? Just delete his name?"

"Yes. It's too big a risk to leave him on. If our officers can't follow the simple filing instructions in the Patriot Act, that leaves us open to lawsuits."

"OK," John Boy said with a quick shrug. He stood up and piled all the papers together. He flicked the switch again and the office wall cleared of smoke. He went back to his three monitors and did a quick eenie-meenie-miney-moe to decide which screen he wanted to use. He opened the Terrorist Watch List and scrolled through the thousands of names until he arrived at Viktor Qu'aro. He placed his cursor at the end of Qu'aro's name and began pressing the delete button on his keyboard.

***

"Are you ready, senator?" Little Dickie's chief of staff poked his head into the senator's office. "They're waiting."

Little Dickie looked over the press statement one last time. He took a big gulp of whiskey and swaggered into the hallway, where the media dog pack was waiting for him. They all began yelling questions at once. "What's your relationship to the Crown Prince?" "Were you aware you were receiving donations from terrorists?" "Is it true you were with the Crown Prince when the terrorists were caught?"

"All right, everybody. Settle down, settle down. I'm gonna answer all your questions, just give me a minute."

The hounds quieted down.

Little Dickie cleared his throat and began, "Several months ago, my super PAC, Dick's Socially Active Citizens PAC, or Dick's SACPAC, began receiving donations from a company in France. As you all know, I am very particular about whom I receive contributions from, and I certainly would not readily accept money from the French. I am aware of what this would do to my reputation as a United States senator. As such, I asked Director-FBI to investigate this company in order to allow me, as a responsible politician, to decide whether or not to accept such donations. When the FBI informed me that this company was connected to someone with a funny name in Atlanta, I encouraged the FBI field office to uncover as much information as possible. Under orders from Director-FBI, who I fully supported in this, the Atlanta field office launched a discreet but highly effective investigation, which uncovered a terrorist cell living in Atlanta, right here in our midst, planning, conniving, plotting an act of such evil, it is unimaginable to God-fearing citizens like you and me." Little Dickie paused for a moment, looking thoughtfully down at the floor.

"You know, before the big attacks on the United States, our intelligence system was in shambles. Our agencies didn't know what to focus on or how to communicate with one another. Just weeks before those horrible attacks, many in our intelligence apparatus were concentrating on superfluous threats, sending us reports on missile defense and Liechtenstein's efforts to build a nuclear weapons program. It's true, we had asked for those reports. But we relied on the intelligence community to tell us we were being sidetracked. We counted on the intelligence community to tell us what we needed to know. And not just by sending us other reports we hadn't asked for with headlines that said, 'Terrorists plan to attack the United States,' but by making us read them. That certainly would have been helpful.

"After that failure on the part of the intelligence community, I am pleased to say I was the driving force behind the creation of the Intelligence Über Director. I envisioned an organization that would help our intelligence agencies coordinate their efforts and cooperate in their analysis in order to allow us to connect the dots and prevent similar attacks from ever happening again. Today, I stand before you, pleased as punch that the agency I created, the IÜD, has functioned exactly as I envisioned. Due to the IÜD's coordinating role, the CYA and FBI worked together, tracking a terrorist from overseas here to our very own hallowed shores, where he was promptly put under surveillance and, in the end, captured before he could execute his heinous plan.

"Ladies and gentlemen of the press, I cannot express how pleased I am to have played such a critical role in this operation. All of us here in Congress get the chance to serve our country. Very few of us get the chance to save it."

The media erupted in applause and Little Dickie began shaking hands with his audience, saying, "Thank you! Thank you! May I remind my constituents that I am up for re-election?"

Within seconds, Senator Dick Head's speech was available on Facebook and his campaign web site. The media printed and broadcast it verbatim as its own story, since they had all forgotten to ask any questions, so overcome were they by Little Dickie's words.

CHAPTER FIFTY-FIVE
CUBA

The smell of mariposa flowers wafted into Omar's prison cell on the sweet Caribbean breeze. He would calm his nerves by listening to the sound of the ocean lapping against the shore, but his reverie would be broken with a single glance at the bars holding him inside. *Where did I go wrong?*

He could not stop himself from going over all the points in his timeline to terror at which he wished he had been more forceful with Zawiki about how the operation should have been carried out. Core Central had taken control and enforced a system on all the Core franchises that was supposed to prevent detection and allow for the smooth execution of operations. Omar had done everything Core Central had asked. He had filled out the forms, gotten the signatures, undergone training, and yet, here he was. "Wearing an orange jumpsuit!" he yelled.

"Psst. It's not orange."

"Who said that?" Omar looked around but saw no one.

"I'm in the cell next door. It's not orange."

"What's not orange?"

"Your jumpsuit. They changed it to clementine a few months ago. I personally don't see a difference, but the men seem to like it. I think they considered calling the color mandarin, but some people wanted to save that for the next war."

"Al-Suqqit!" A guard yelled from the corridor as a metal door slammed behind him. Omar could hear his neighbor scurry toward the back of his cell. The guard unlocked Omar's cell door and led him out. "Your lawyer's here."

Omar said nothing but his mind raced. He didn't have a lawyer that he knew of. He was brought to a small room with a small table and two chairs. A distinguished looking gentleman got up from one of the chairs and shook Omar's hand.

"Mr. al-Suqqit, it is so nice to meet you. I'm Phillip Linkins, your lawyer. Please, sit down." The gentleman gave the guards a barely perceptible nod and they left the room without a word.

Omar waited for Phillip Linkins to speak.

Linkins reached into the inside pocket of his blue linen jacket and pulled out a hefty Cuban cigar. He slid it under his nose and inhaled deeply. With a glance at the no smoking sign posted on the wall, he lit the cigar with the manifested pleasure of a man who knows impunity and puffed three times before looking hard at Omar.

"It was your phone, Mr. al-Suqqit. And the credit card you were using. They had both been used in previous operations. The FBI was able to track everything you did with those two pieces of information." He took another big puff. "Your phone had been used by a sleeper cell in Buffalo that was rounded up last year. The credit card traced back to a terror plot in Malaysia a few months ago."

Omar sat silently across from Linkins. It made sense, what he said. But could the desk warriors at Caliphate Crossing really have been so naïve? He had known about the cell in Buffalo. They were arrested after trying to dash without paying for a lap dance they had received. Had Core Central not destroyed those tainted phones? Did someone really pass him one of those phones, rather than go through the admittedly arduous process of getting a clean one? Omar understood it was time consuming and not all that interesting to stand in an AT&T store for an afternoon, but wasn't that an effort they were ready to exert to ensure the safety of his operation? And the credit card? No one thought to close that account after the Malaysia plot was discovered? Core Central was supposed to deconflict exactly these kinds of details, he thought.

"We're going to move you to a federal prison back in the United States, Mr. al-Suqqit."

This pulled Omar out of his thoughts and he gave Linkins a questioning look.

"I think we have a good case to get you released. This won't even make it to trial."

"I heard prison in America is terrible," Omar said. "Everyone finds God and tries to radicalize you."

"You're already radicalized, Mr. al-Suqqit. That shouldn't be a problem."

"No, radicalized the other way. I hear they have evangelicals."

"I don't think you'll be there long. Please, let the system work for you."

Omar was led back to his cell to gather his few belongings. He looked around the tiny cement space and picked up his IKEA catalog to take with him. Before he knew it, he had shed his clementine jumpsuit and was on a plane heading back to Atlanta.

CHAPTER FIFTY-SIX
WASHINGTON, DC

Victor got out of the shower at Vanessa's apartment and felt clean for the first time in days. He still wasn't quite sure how or why he had been let out of jail—not that he should have been there in the first place. He had been sitting on the same bench alternating between hitting his head on the wall and smacking his forehead with the palm of his hand for two days when, with no obvious impetus, an Atlanta police officer unlocked the cell and told him to go. He did, without asking any questions that might land him back in the cell. He had walked out and not looked back.

He turned on the television and Vanessa sat down beside him. A young female talking head with glossy lips and bouncy blonde hair was standing outside the Atlanta federal courthouse. A mob of people was yelling and causing a commotion in the background.

"The judge ordering that this hearing remain closed given all the media interest," the glimmering talking head said. "The accused, Omar al-Suqqit, taking former National Security Adviser Phillip Linkins as his lawyer. Mr. Linkins insisting his client is innocent and denying that his own close connections to people in

Washington pose any conflict of interest. Mr. Linkins, of course, being a close friend of former Senator and past CYA Director Richard Redd, Senior."

"Why do all the talking heads have the same haircut?" Victor asked Vanessa.

"Why do they all speak in gerunds?" asked Vanessa.

"Wait a minute. Wait a minute." The talking head was holding a hand to her ear, listening to a voice coming in through her earpiece. "We're being told Phillip Linkins will be making a statement here any moment. The hearing being dismissed, right now, as I speak to you. And Omar al-Suqqit's lawyer agreeing to make a statement. That should be happening any moment now." The mob behind her broke into a frenzy as the lawyer strutted out of the courthouse and down the stairs, stopping midway to allow the microphones to come to him. The glossy talking head jumped into the fray, pushing a microphone through the gaggle and into Phillip Linkins's face.

"I stand before you a content man. I am content because today we reconfirmed that we are a nation of laws. I have said this from the beginning and I reiterate it now, my client, Omar al-Suqqit, was a victim. A victim of Big Brother gone awry. A victim of illegal surveillance. A victim of illegal wire-tapping. A victim of a predatory credit card company. A victim, pure and simple. We cannot let our fear undermine our values as a country. Today, I am content because the system worked. The system worked!" Linkins thrust a fist into the air. "The judge has agreed that such illegal maneuverings on the part of our law enforcement authorities—think about that a moment." He paused and looked at the media pack. "Law enforcement authorities, the very people who should be fighting to uphold our constitution. The judge agreed that their illegal maneuverings violated my client's civil rights. As such, the judge has dismissed this case. I have spoken personally with Director-FBI, who has assured me that the people responsible for this will face disciplinary action. I will not be taking any questions. Thank you."

Victor and Vanessa couldn't speak. They couldn't move. They couldn't believe. Vanessa was the first finally to break the silence.

"Lovely."

"That's what you get for stopping a terrorist just before he sets off a massive bomb. How could you?"

"We should have let him go through with it. Then his guilt would have been confirmed."

She got up and started getting dressed.

"Where are you going?"

"I better go face the music."

CHAPTER FIFTY-SEVEN
CALIPHATE CROSSING, RUBBLESTAN

Omar felt a little shell-shocked to find himself on a luxury private plane, when just hours before he had been sitting in a cold, hard, gray prison cell in a federal penitentiary, being lectured by a large white man with tattoos about Jesus' views on homosexuality and soap sharing. Now, he was back in his *shalwar kameez* and nervously fingering his prayer beads. He was sorry not to have been able to see Leyla before he was whisked to a car and to the airport, but his lawyer had informed him that, although she had had her student visa revoked, she had been freed and was en route to Nuakabatu.

"Don't worry," Linkins had told him. "She's got a bright future ahead of her on TV after that martyr video."

At first, Omar was told he would be flying back to the DRZ, as well. But at the last minute, Linkins informed Omar that he had been summoned to Rubblestan. Omar could only imagine what Zawiki had in mind, calling him all the way to Rubblestan. His operation had failed, so whatever reason Zawiki had, it couldn't be good.

Caliphate Crossing was buzzing with energy when Omar walked in. Other fighters went about their plotting, unaware of Omar's plight. As he saw them move through Teahadi as if in a factory, he realized he was one small cog in a huge wheel of freedom fighting. Other plots were being planned. Some would succeed; others would fail. But the Core kept them all going.

He arrived in the conference cave before the others and took a seat on the rug to wait. More motivational posters had been hung up on the walls. One read **TEAMWORK** and showed a man helping attach his friend's explosive belt. Another read **ACHIEVEMENT** under a photograph of a severed, bloody arm.

Omar could hear voices down the corridor and soon a group of young kids came in the conference cave and sat down. Omar couldn't help but think about how these young fighters lacked professionalism, lounging this way and that on the rug and loading their tea with sugar. One female even let her headscarf slip almost entirely off her head.

He pined for the old days of the Brotherhood. He felt that, although his group had been small, it had been more maneuverable and easy to control, and his fighters had always made sure good tradecraft was a priority, even if that meant blowing up fewer things. He had wanted to expand, it was true, but now he wondered if bigger maybe was not better. These young fighters, Omar thought, they had joined the Core ranks in the midst of the Great Enemy's Total War on Terror, just as Core Central had begun consolidating global operations. All they knew was war. They were being trained to operate in this war environment. Tradecraft had become a side note, he was convinced. That was why so many attempts had failed, with keys left in the car bombs that only smoked but never blew up. And that, he was sure, was why one of these warrior trainees sitting in front of him now had given him a phone and a credit card that were tainted by other operations.

Zawiki rolled into the conference room on a donkey cart. He was even fatter than Omar remembered. He held a giant cup of soda in one hand and was adjusting the photograph of his goat, which he'd attached to the basket on the side of the cart. When he saw Omar, he smiled brightly and tried to jump off the cart to greet him, but his pudginess got in the way and instead he slid like a giant slug to the edge of the cart and slithered down the side.

"We're glad to see you, Omar. Sorry it isn't under better circumstances." The young warriors regarded Zawiki with an almost idolatrous gaze, which was ironic, Omar noted, given where the Core usually stood on idolatry. "At least your lawyer managed to clean up your mess in Atlanta. The Crown Prince did well to hire him."

"The Crown Prince got me my lawyer?"

"That is correct, Omar. The Crown Prince is well connected in Washington, and Linkins is the best. You know he was national security adviser? Good people. And good connections. A good combination. I helped, of course, from my desk here."

Omar tried to give him an enthusiastic smile but couldn't.

Zawiki turned to the rest of the group. "Now, everyone, let's talk through where things went wrong with this operation. That's the point of this meeting, to review the failure and see if we could have stopped it from failing had some different decisions been made."

"It was the phone and the credit card," Omar said. "There's nothing to discuss. Who assigned me that phone and that credit card?" He looked at the young desk warriors, who looked at Zawiki. "The phone and the credit card had been used before. The phone had been used by a sleeper cell in Buffalo that had been rounded up by the FBI, and the credit card went to a company connected to another company that exported terror. How did this happen?" Omar could not hide his anger.

"Calm down, now, Omar," Zawiki said. "Let's not point fingers here. We don't know exactly what happened."

"We do know what happened. Someone was either too lazy or too stupid to get me a clean phone and a clean credit card."

One of the young warriors spoke up. "Khaled found the phone and credit card in a drawer in his desk. The guy in finance was on leave to take a third wife and Khaled couldn't get a different credit card in time. The brother who procures phones and checks them for security was at an off-site."

"You see?" Zawiki said to Omar, as if that solved everything.

"No, I don't see."

"This was a systemic failure. Khaled was showing initiative. We don't want to penalize him for that. The finance person being away to take a third wife, well, that is a regulation we cannot claw back, it's part of what makes this such a nice place to work and accounts for our low attrition rate, not counting the Martyr Program, of course. Those statistics are quite different. As for the mobile phone person, we highly encourage new training. That is what keeps us fresh and creative. So, you see, it was a systemic failure."

"Specific individuals didn't do their jobs. How can you characterize that as a systemic failure? You're not going to hold anyone accountable?" Omar almost yelled. "I could have rotted in prison, and no one gets held accountable?"

"But you're not in prison, and how can we hold an individual accountable when it's the system that failed? Ahmed, take this down," he said to the young desk warrior. "Given recent systemic failures that led to the ill success of our operation in Atlanta, Core Central has developed the following regulations that shall apply to all Core franchise operations." Ahmed was writing down Zawiki's words as quickly as he could. Zawiki continued, "First, no Core franchise shall use any credit cards from Malaysia, nor shall they open shell companies there. In fact, no more Malaysia. Period. Requests for exemptions may be submitted to Core Central Leadership, who shall read these requests for exemptions on alternate Tuesdays. Second, no more phones. Falcons only for communications."

"What about communications between cells in Europe or the United States?" asked Ahmed. "Falcons might stand out there."

"Falcons only!" Zawiki shouted. "Lastly," he turned to face Omar. "Purchases at IKEA shall be limited to five percent of an operation's total budget." He turned back to Ahmed. "We're done here. Write that up and send it to all Core franchises. Thanks for coming everyone." The desk warriors got up to leave. Omar sat a moment longer, seething. As he was about to get up, Zawiki stopped him. "Omar, one last thing."

Omar clenched his fists in an attempt to control his anger.

"I'm afraid we can't let you go back to the Democratic Republic of Zuzu."

"Why?"

"Obviously you've been compromised. You would be a liability to any plot."

"What am I supposed to do?"

"We've set up a desk for you down in the stalactite corridor."

"Completely underground?"

"I think you'll find the conditions quite cozy, once you get accustomed to the lack of light and the smell of soggy goat hair. All right then, excuse me. I have a meeting with the rest of Core Leadership to discuss what changes we can make to ensure such a systemic failure never happens again." Omar stayed sitting on the rug while Zawiki waddled to his cart and hefted himself up onto it, like a walrus getting out of its pool at the zoo.

CHAPTER FIFTY-EIGHT
WASHINGTON, DC

Victor and Vanessa sat down for dinner in her apartment for a last meal together. Victor had to go to Director the following day and then would fly back to Pigallo in the evening to start the fight against terrorism anew.

"It was a slap on the wrist, really," Vanessa told Victor in between bites. "Director-FBI couldn't really discipline me too much, after that motivational speech from Senator Dick Head about how he saved the world. I was warned not to rock the boat and to keep my head down."

"I'm sorry if I got you into trouble."

"Please. We did the right thing. The system worked, right? Isn't that what Dick Head said?"

"The system didn't work. A few of us in the system did the right thing. That's all."

"Speaking of Senator Dick Head. His approval ratings jumped so high after his speech that he's thinking of running for president."

"You're joking."

"He wants to stick it to his dad, who never made it to the White House. Guess who he's hired as his foreign policy adviser?"

"Do tell," said Victor.

"A certain Walid al-Mann, CEO of one French company named Pistache."

"You're kidding me."

"I wish I were. And get this. Walid is a nephew of, can you guess it?"

"Don't tell me," Victor cringed in anticipation.

"The Crown Prince of Ombudai. Isn't Washington glorious?" Vanessa took a long drink from her wine glass. "Of course, I'm not supposed to know any of this."

Victor laughed. "Of course not. And you won't be looking further into any of it. You wouldn't want to rock the boat."

"Exactly. I might face disciplinary action if I did." Victor knew from the way she smiled at him she had no intention of not looking into it. "It's all unbelievable, isn't it?" she asked.

Victor shook his head. "It's actually completely believable."

CHAPTER FIFTY-NINE
CALIPHATE CROSSING, RUBBLESTAN

O mar's cubicle in the stalactite corridor was dank and cold. He couldn't get past the idea that he could no longer be operational. He had helped found the Brotherhood and had looked to make it an international player. But in so doing, he had brought his own demise. Now here he was, in the bowels of Caliphate Crossing, shuffling and stapling papers and taking breaks to visit Teahadi four times a day. When he caught himself considering what type of frame would best suit a cute photograph he had of himself with his new pet camel and how he could hang it up inside his cubicle, he had to splash cold water on his face and remind himself that he was still a master warrior, even if Zawiki was trying to take that away by hiding him down here.

A new cable came in on his computer. He didn't really feel like reading it but at least it would help pass the time until five o'clock. He poured a little more sugar into his tea as he read, slipped a cardboard ring around the cup so he wouldn't burn his fingers, and took a sip. He heard a commotion down the corridor and stood up to go investigate. He got out of his chair slowly, since his legs were rather numb, and he took a few small steps before reaching his normal stride.

In the conference cave, a number of Caliphate Crossing-based fighters were celebrating with fig cake and cherry juice. A dozen of them were fist bumping and backslapping the subject of the celebration. Omar leaned in for a better look and saw Zawiki hugging his fighters. His beard was stained red from the cherry juice and Omar thought he saw half an empty pistachio shell clinging to it. Ahmed came up the main corridor behind Omar and squeezed past him to get to the celebration. "Are you coming?" Ahmed asked him.

"What's the occasion?" Omar asked.

"Dr. Zawiki got promoted! He's now Core Central's number three!"

Omar smiled. "God is great!" he yelled. He walked back toward his desk. "God is great."

CHAPTER SIXTY
WASHINGTON, DC

Victor waded through the parked cars, forcibly willing himself to go to Director. He swiped his badge and went down the escalators to the main floor. He looked at the artifacts placed around the atrium, marking Director's past achievements. Behind a glass case stood a mannequin dressed in a North Face fleece and khaki cargo pants, with a pair of dark Ray-Ban sunglasses peeking out from behind the *keffiyeh* wrapped around its head. The label on the case read, "The uniform of a typical undercover officer in Rubblestan."

In a corner was a new photo Victor had not seen before. He walked over to it and observed the picture of a sleek building, newly constructed, in front of a backdrop of mountains he recognized. He looked at the caption: "The new, $700 million base built in Rubblestan, complete with an Olympic-size pool, three tennis courts, and an aromatherapy shop. The base was compromised before any personnel could move in and was given as a gift to the Rubblestan government."

Out in the courtyard, Victor saw that a ceremony was underway, likely acknowledging another accomplishment on the part of one of Director's officers. He went outside to listen and saw John Boy standing on a small platform with Director speaking at a podium next to him.

"Not all of our officers go above and beyond their duty. But this officer, John Boy, has given the words 'Dedication to the Mission' new meaning. I am honored to present to him the rare Freedom Medal, to express our gratitude for his tireless work in dismantling and bringing down the FNU LNU terrorist network." John Boy grinned like a child who had just been handed a huge ice cream cone with sprinkles on top. "I am pleased to announce that he is being promoted to head of targeting for all of our counterterrorism efforts. John Boy, I thank you. Your nation thanks you." Director then pinned the Freedom Medal on the trainee who had sent Victor off on a mistaken rendition and who had, apparently, single handedly brought down a group of terrorists with no names.

Victor went back inside and walked to the office that worked on the Brotherhood, now the Core in the Desert. Kinesha had moved again and was the gatekeeper for this office. She was tapping her long nails on her desk and smiling dreamily at a burly man standing above her. Victor heard the man say, "What a great photo of your cats, Kinesha."

Victor walked up behind the man. "What the fuck are you doing here, Zed?"

Zed turned around and wrapped Victor in a bear hug. "Oh, Victor." He released Victor then stepped back to take a better look. "You look like shit."

"Thanks."

"Director called me back to ask me why we didn't capture al-Suqqit before he ever made it to the States."

"We tried to. In Rubblestan. Director refused."

"You and I know that, Victor. But these things are easily forgotten. It's not like they're written down and stored forever in a database where we could easily recall them."

"Your sarcasm is soothing, Zed. I've missed you."

"I've got more for you. Come in the conference room."

Victor followed Zed and was surprised to see a group of people attacking a cake. They applauded when they saw Victor.

"What is this?" Victor asked.

Zed quieted everyone down and shouted over the room. "Dear, Victor. I am pleased to announce that I was able to convince Director that we in Pigallo played a small part in catching al-Suqqit and stopping him from blowing up a major American city. A minor accomplishment, but an accomplishment nonetheless. I also told Director that you specifically, Victor, were indispensable in capturing one of the most wanted terrorists in the world. Again, a minor accomplishment, but one I feel deserves some kind of recognition. Even if that terrorist was later set free. Just proves the judicial system works as well as the IÜD system. Now, I first told Director you should get an Exceptional Performance Award for your role in bringing down a terror cell."

"Oh, Zed. Say it ain't so! You got me an EPA? Please tell me this will appear in next week's Director highlights."

"I'm afraid not, Victor. Director felt it wasn't right to give you an EPA, since technically speaking you were on leave at the time of al-Suqqit's capture. Director thought it was a little irresponsible of you to take a vacation in the middle of the Total War on Terror."

Victor snapped his fingers and said, "That'll teach me."

"I did manage to secure this for your outstanding contribution to fighting global terror." Zed triumphantly held a piece of paper high up over his head.

"It can't possibly be true."

"It is, my dear boy, it is." Zed handed the paper to Victor while announcing to the room, "A twenty-five-dollar gift certificate to the Cheesecake Factory. Read it and weep, Victor. Read it and weep."

"It does make me feel like crying," Victor said.

The people in the room congratulated Victor and handed out cake. They slapped him on the back, shook his hand while grinning, and wished him well in his future endeavors fighting terrorism. As Victor was finishing a piece of cake, Joseph the Support Officer walked in. Zed and Victor gave each other a confused look.

"Sorry to break up the festivities," Joseph said. "But I heard someone just got a Cheesecake Factory gift certificate?"

Victor, holding the gift certificate, hid his hands behind his back. Joseph turned to him. "I'm afraid I have to take that back."

"What's going on, Joseph?" Zed asked.

"Director's orders. We're taking back all non-monetary awards. See, when an employee gets a monetary award, it's included in that employee's paycheck and thus is taxed appropriately. These gift certificates are essentially cash, only the recipient is never taxed. That's not fair. Director is abolishing all non-monetary awards. For the ones that have already been given, we have to ask for them back. Sorry. No free dessert." Joseph put his hand out to Victor. "But we really appreciate your hard work."

Victor clutched the piece of paper even tighter in his fist and pulled it as far away from Joseph as he could. He clapped Zed's shoulder and gave him a little nod and then walked out of the department and down the long corridor. He stepped on the escalator, still holding the piece of paper and staring straight ahead. He got off the escalator, walked over to the security guard's desk and handed him his badge. He walked down the main hallway, holding his head high. He exited through the sliding glass doors, ripped up the crumpled gift certificate, and threw the pieces into the air. As they exploded into a burst of snow and floated away on the wind, Victor walked away and disappeared into the endless rows of parked cars.

ACKNOWLEDGEMENTS

Writing this book began as a catharsis. For years, while most people watched an official narrative of the "War on Terror" unfolding in all its inglorious grimness across the global stage, I sat in my little cubicle and witnessed absurdity. Watching a war on terror from behind the curtain is a bit like watching sausage being made: ridiculous amounts of random parts all being shoved together and hoping it will work, and the inclusion of an asshole here and there. I will let the reader speculate where things lie on the truth spectrum, but I will say Mark Twain was right: Truth is, indeed, stranger than fiction.

I have many people to thank for their help and support in bringing this story to the printed page.

A huge shout out to the Q-town writing group: Wes, Howard, Marta, and Amanda, who knew the promise of wine and cheese was enough to motivate me to write something. Thanks for your feedback and encouragement and—the best part—your laughter while you read. I blame the altitude!

I have to give special thanks to Amanda, who has been one of my biggest cheerleaders (although she will detest being called that). She encouraged me to write (anything!) and she read more drafts than any human should ever have to. She also proved a sturdy and reliable—and willing!—sounding board for this and many other projects, both professional and personal.

Elizabeth Stein provided invaluable feedback and editing and remained patient when I pushed back over having to cut jokes. The manuscript is much tighter thanks to her efforts. Sage Sweetwater helped edit an early draft and has been a stalwart supporter in helping me build my platform and get the word out.

Tammy read an early draft and provided useful feedback and guidance. She was also a constant source of encouragement during a period of seemingly unending rejection. She soothed the blow with excellent wine and laughter, and I thank her for it.

Many friends and former colleagues have helped me along the way, as well. Some know the important role they played (or inspired!); others might not know how their actions or words influenced this book. To my friends still out in the cold, I hope this book provides some comic relief next time Headquarters refuses to release your asset funds because you did not ref all sixteen case cables when explaining your two-dollar disbursement on your last SDR, and their warning that any release of funds must be coordinated by thirty-two individuals, all of whom are on flextime or down at the Amish Quilt Competition in the atrium, even though your asset meeting in a denied area is tomorrow. Stay safe.

I, of course, have to thank Mom and Dad, for their endless encouragement—to write, to travel, to challenge myself—for their positive example to do what makes you happy, and for their love.

My brother, too, has consistently pushed me to do what I thought was beyond my abilities and is always ready to help (or just listen to me complain). Additionally, his courage and humor through trying times were a lesson in grace that will stay with me always. My son makes me want to do and achieve great things. I hope this book encourages him to follow his own path.

Lastly, I have to thank my husband. He knows why.

ABOUT THE AUTHOR

Alex Finley is a former officer of the CIA's Directorate of Operations, where she served in West Africa and Europe. Before becoming a bureaucrat living large off the system, she chased puffy white men around Washington, DC, as a member of the wild dog pack better known as the Washington media elite. Her writing has appeared in Slate, Reductress, Funny or Die, and other publications.

Follow her on Twitter: @alexzfinley

alexzfinley.com